THE
CANALS OF
VENICE

BUILDING
HISTORY
SERIES

THE
CANALS OF
VENICE

TITLES IN THE BUILDING HISTORY SERIES INCLUDE:

Alcatraz
The Atom Bomb
The Eiffel Tower
The Golden Gate Bridge
The Great Wall of China
The Holy City of Jerusalem
The Hoover Dam
Machu Picchu
The Medieval Castle
The Medieval Cathedral
Mount Rushmore
The New York Subway System
The Palace of Versailles
The Panama Canal
The Parthenon of Ancient Greece
The Pyramids of Giza
The Roman Colosseum
Roman Roads and Aqueducts
The Russian Kremlin
Shakespeare's Globe
The Sistine Chapel
The Space Shuttle
The Statue of Liberty
Stonehenge
The Suez Canal
The Taj Mahal
The Titanic
The Tower of Pisa
The Transcontinental Railroad
The Vatican
The Viking Longship
The White House
The World Trade Center

BUILDING
HISTORY
SERIES

THE
CANALS OF
VENICE

by Marcia Amidon Lüsted

LUCENT
BOOKS®

THOMSON
™
GALE

San Diego • Detroit • New York • San Francisco • Cleveland
New Haven, Conn. • Waterville, Maine • London • Munich

© 2004 by Lucent Books. Lucent Books is an imprint of The Gale Group, Inc.,
a division of Thomson Learning, Inc.

Lucent Books® and Thomson Learning™ are trademarks used herein under license.

For more information, contact
Lucent Books
27500 Drake Rd.
Farmington Hills, MI 48331-3535
Or you can visit our Internet site at http://www.gale.com

LIBRARY OF CONGRESS CATALOGING-IN-PUBLICATION DATA

Lüsted, Marcia Amidon.
    The canals of Venice / by Marcia Amidon Lüsted.
        v. cm. — (Building history)
Includes bibliographical references and index.
Contents: Canals of Venice—Origins of the city—Structure of Venice—Heart of the city—Building a palace in Venice—Venice in peril.
    ISBN 1-59018-341-X (hardback : alk. paper)
    1. Venice (Italy)—History—Juvenile literature. [1. Venice (Italy)—History.] I. Title.
II. Building history series.
    DG676.L87 2004
    945'.31—dc22
                                                                2003012905

Printed in the United States of America

CONTENTS

Foreword

Throughout history, as civilizations have evolved and prospered, each has produced unique buildings and architectural styles. Combining the need for both utility and artistic expression, a society's buildings, particularly its large-scale public structures, often reflect the individual character traits that distinguish it from other societies. In a very real sense, then, buildings express a society's values and unique characteristics in tangible form. As scholar Anita Abramovitz comments in her book *People and Spaces*, "Our ways of living and thinking—our habits, needs, fear of enemies, aspirations, materialistic concerns, and religious beliefs—have influenced the kinds of spaces that we build and that later surround and include us."

That specific types and styles of structures constitute an outward expression of the spirit of an individual people or era can be seen in the diverse ways that various societies have built palaces, fortresses, tombs, churches, government buildings, sports arenas, public works, and other such monuments. The ancient Greeks, for instance, were a supremely rational people who originated Western philosophy and science, including the atomic theory and the realization that the Earth is a sphere. Their public buildings, epitomized by Athens's magnificent Parthenon temple, were equally rational, emphasizing order, harmony, reason, and above all, restraint.

By contrast, the Romans, who conquered and absorbed the Greek lands, were a highly practical people preoccupied with acquiring and wielding power over others. The Romans greatly admired and readily copied elements of Greek architecture, but modified and adapted them to their own needs. "Roman genius was called into action by the enormous practical needs of a world empire," wrote historian Edith Hamilton. "Rome met them magnificently. Buildings tremendous, indomitable, amphitheaters where eighty thousand could watch a spectacle, baths where three thousand could bathe at the same time."

In medieval Europe, God heavily influenced and motivated the people, and religion permeated all aspects of society, molding people's worldviews and guiding their everyday actions. That spiritual mindset is reflected in the most important medieval structure—the Gothic cathedral—which, in a sense, was a model of heavenly cities. As scholar Anne Fremantle so elegantly phrases it, the cathedrals were "harmonious elevations of stone and glass reaching up to heaven to seek and receive the light [of God]."

Our more secular modern age, in contrast, is driven by the realities of a global economy, advanced technology, and mass communications. Responding to the needs of international trade and the growth of cities housing millions of people, today's builders construct engineering marvels, among them towering skyscrapers of steel and glass, mammoth marine canals, and huge and elaborate rapid transit systems, all of which would have left their ancestors, even the Romans, awestruck.

In examining some of humanity's greatest edifices, Lucent Books' Building History series recognizes this close relationship between a society's historical character and its buildings. Each volume in the series begins with a historical sketch of the people who erected the edifice, exploring their major achievements as well as the beliefs, customs, and societal needs that dictated the variety, functions, and styles of their buildings. A detailed explanation of how the selected structure was conceived, designed, and built, to the extent that this information is known, makes up the majority of the volume.

Each volume in the Lucent Building History series also includes several special features that are useful tools for additional research. A chronology of important dates gives students an overview, at a glance, of the evolution and use of the structure described. Sidebars create a broader context by adding further details on some of the architects, engineers, and construction tools, materials, and methods that made each structure a reality, as well as the social, political, and/or religious leaders and movements that inspired its creation. Useful maps help the reader locate the nations, cities, streets, and individual structures mentioned in the text; and numerous diagrams and pictures illustrate tools and devices that bring to life various stages of construction. Finally, each volume contains two bibliographies, one for student research, the other listing works the author consulted in compiling the book.

Taken as a whole, these volumes, covering diverse ancient and modern structures, constitute not only a valuable research tool, but also a tribute to the human spirit, a fascinating exploration of the dreams, skills, ingenuity, and dogged determination of the great peoples who shaped history.

Important Dates in the Building of the Canals of Venice

421
Venice is founded on March 25, St. Mark's Day, after the patron saint of Venice.

726
The first documented doge begins his rule.

828
Venetian merchants steal the body of Saint Mark from Alexandria.

1095
The First Crusade to reclaim the Holy Land from the Muslims.

1171
The six districts (*sestieri*) of Venice are founded.

1202–1204
Venetians participate in the Fourth Crusade.

1295
Marco Polo returns to Venice after a twenty-five-year voyage.

1348
The Black Plague begins and about half the population of Venice dies.

1000	1100	1200	1300	1400

1000
Doge Orseolo rids the Adriatic Sea of pirates and conducts the first Marriage to the Sea ceremony.

832
The first Basilica of Saint Mark is completed.

814
Work begins on the first doge's palace.

452
Attila the Hun invades Italy and plunders Venice and the Veneto region.

1104
Venice's Arsenale shipyard is founded.

1204
Venice participates in the conquest of the city of Constantinople and brings home the four bronze horses of Saint Mark's Basilica.

1309
The present doge's palace is begun.

1434
The Ca'd'Oro is finished.

2003
The MOSE project receives government approval and construction is begun on the mobile gates, expected to take eight years to finish.

1630
Another plague epidemic reduces the Venetian population to its lowest number in 250 years.

1866
Venice becomes part of the kingdom of Italy.

1708
The winter is so bitter that the lagoon freezes and Venetians can walk to the mainland.

1902
The campanile in the Piazza San Marco collapses.

1925–1973
Groundwater is pumped from beneath the city of Venice for industrial use.

1797
Napoléon invades Venice and the Venetian Republic ends.

1500	1600	1700	1800	1900

1755
Casanova is imprisoned in the Leads.

1988
A prototype gate for the MOSE flood control system is tested in the lagoon.

1967
A deep channel is cut through the lagoon for petroleum tankers.

1966
Venice experiences its most severe flood.

1846
The railway causeway links Venice to the mainland for the first time.

INTRODUCTION

Venice, Italy, is located on more than one hundred small islands in the middle of a lagoon on the shores of the Adriatic Sea, roughly halfway between the cities of Verona and Trieste in northern Italy. Venice is one of the most recognizable cities in the world, largely because its seawater canals take the place of streets, and boats replace cars or trucks as the primary means of transportation. Other cities in the world have historically used canals for transportation, but most of these have been altered to accommodate car traffic. Only Venice has remained a city that is almost totally dependent on the canals and the sea for daily commerce and commuting. The Venice of today is a mix of contradictions: modern industrial-commercial center, major tourist attraction, artistic and architectural treasure, and site of more than a thousand years of history. It is thus a city struggling with issues of identity as it decides whether to remain a real, working urban center populated by real Venetians or become virtually a high-priced amusement park for tourists.

VENICE OF THE PAST

According to tradition, Venice was founded in A.D. 421 on a lagoon as a refuge for mainland dwellers to escape the invading barbarian armies that would soon roam the area after the fall of the Roman Empire. As Venice grew, it established its own government, proclaiming itself a republic in 697, and began to trade with cities in the East. Its strategic location and skillful merchants made it the center of a trading and shipbuilding empire that lasted nearly a thousand years and brought incredible wealth to the city and its worldly inhabitants. Because of its trade relationships with the Eastern empires, Venice developed as a city that incorporated both Eastern and Western attitudes and influences in architecture, dress, and popular culture.

Because of its island location, Venice was accessible only by sea until the construction of a railroad bridge after Napoléon I conquered the republic in 1797. This relative isolation helped the city to remain independent from the rest of Europe and fostered a unique Venetian character. In 1866 the former city-state joined the kingdom of Italy, which eventually became the country of Italy as it is today, but Venice retained its sense of separation from the rest of Europe and the mystique that has drawn visitors for centuries.

VENICE OF THE IMAGINATION

For most people, the name Venice brings to mind gondolas floating on the Grand Canal and elaborate palaces lining the water. Known as La Serenissima, "the most serene" or "the noblest," Venice has fascinated travelers since its earliest days, offering endless inspiration for artists, writers, musicians, and filmmakers. Even as the city began to decay after the fall of the Venetian Republic in 1797, tourism thrived, becoming one of its major industries. The romantic image of Venice as a gorgeous city virtually floating on the ocean draws people there from all over the world, but the canals of Venice and other historic features overshadow the city's real needs and problems, such as adequate facilities for its inhabitants, jobs, schools, and affordable housing.

VENICE AND THE FUTURE

With the severe floods that engulfed Venice in 1966, the world began to realize that the romance and historical value of the city were not going to last without intervention. Venice was famous

Venice's famous gondolas, palaces, and canals have beckoned tourists for centuries.

for her canals, but these canals and the rising tides of the ocean were destroying her buildings, most of which were built so closely alongside the original canals that their foundations essentially became the canal walls. Organizations from all over the world stepped in to save Venice's historic buildings, as well as to try to solve its environmental problems. Complicated issues of environmental and physical restoration have only just begun to be addressed. Venice, however, has choices to make for its future. Either steps must be taken to enable Venetians to live and work in the city, providing necessary jobs, housing, and services, or the city will become an expensive showplace for the thousands of tourists who come there every day during the summer months. Venice is struggling with its identity, caught between the past and the present, with the echoes of a long, proud history still evident everywhere in the city but with the urgent needs of the modern world becoming more pressing. Balancing these two identities of Venice is one of the most difficult issues it faces today.

The enduring fascination of Venice in the world's imagination can be glimpsed in the words of travel writer Jan Morris:

> The glory of the place lies in the grand fact of Venice herself: the brilliance and strangeness of her history, the wide melancholy lagoon that surrounds her, the convoluted sea-splendor that keeps her, to this day, unique among the cities. When at last you leave these waters, pack away your straw hat and swing out to sea, all the old dazzle of Venice will linger in your mind; and her smell of mud, incense, fish, age, filth and velvet will hang around your nostrils; and the soft lap of her back-canals will echo in your ears; and wherever you go in life you will feel somewhere over your shoulder, a pink, castellated, shimmering presence, the domes and riggings and crooked pinnacles of the Serenissima.[1]

This romantic vision of Venice must be contrasted with the modern industrial and shipping area of Marghera, where Venetians are relocating from their ancestral city in order to find affordable housing and jobs. Venice has always been a city of commerce and industry, prospering while it defended itself from the world. Only by exploring the ways in which the city evolved into what it is today can the world hope to assist Venice as it struggles to define a new twenty-first-century identity.

THE ORIGINS OF
THE CITY

Across the great plain that makes up northern Italy, four rivers descend from the mountain ranges of the eastern Alps and the Dolomites: the Adige, the Brenta, the Piave, and the Tagliamento. These rivers make their way to the Adriatic Sea and create estuaries where the rivers' waters meet the sea, dumping mud, sand, shale, and other sediments that have been carried along by their currents. Long ago, the river estuaries created a flat, muddy marshland at the northern tip of the Adriatic Sea, with a lagoon of shallow water separated from the sea itself by a thin strip of narrow sandbanks and reefs known as *lidi*. This lagoon was a mixture of salt- and freshwater, with a few deep channels that could be navigated by boat, and a great many small sandbars and islands of mud and reeds.

It is this geographical area that would one day become the city of Venice. Difficult to approach even by foot, it would seem the least likely spot to construct a city, unless the city was intended to be unapproachable. As travel writer John Julius Norwich asks, "Who in their right mind would build a village, far less a town or city, on a cluster of soggy shoals and sandbanks rising from a malarial, malodorous lagoon?" [2]

THE END OF THE ROMAN EMPIRE

Around A.D. 400 this marshy lagoon was near the edge of many Roman settlements. In the vicinity were two important Roman roads and four major Roman towns—Aquileia, Concordia, Padua, and Altinum—as well as a number of fishing villages and many vacation villas for wealthy Roman families. The age of the domination of the Roman Empire, however, was coming to a close in the 400s. As Roman influence and strength dissolved, waves of barbarians swept across the region. Groups of invaders such as the Goths, Avars, and Herulians invaded the area, stealing and destroying crops and homes. The Lombards, a Germanic tribe, invaded the area with the intention of settling there permanently. But the most famous of these barbarian invaders were the Huns, under the command of the warlord king Attila. The Huns were horsemen and archers, but they had none of the civilized habits of the Romans, according to the Roman historian Ammianus Marcellinus:

> And though [the Huns] do just bear the likeness of men (of a very ugly pattern), they are so little advanced in civilization that they make no use of fire, nor any kind of relish, in the preparation of their food, but feed upon the roots which they find in the fields, and the half-raw flesh of any sort of animal. I say half-raw, because they give it a kind of cooking by placing it between their own thighs and the backs of their horses.[3]

Attila himself was even rumored to have eaten the flesh of his own sons. True or not, his reputation was so fearsome that when he invaded the Veneto region, as the lagoon area was known, the Roman inhabitants fled their cities and farms for safety and took refuge on the islands of the lagoon. Only those familiar with the area knew how to navigate the hidden channels of deeper water to get to the islands, and the barbarian horsemen could not follow them. The area appeared to be so desolate that most invaders were not even tempted to approach it.

At first, the Romans would flee to the lagoon during times of invasion and then return to their homes afterward. But as time went on and the invasions continued, many locals left the mainland permanently and built homes on the lagoon islands, sometimes displacing the fishermen who had originally settled there.

THE LAGOON ISLANDS

The islands of the lagoon form an archipelago, or chain of islets, and Venice was built on this archipelago, with the mainland shore two miles to the west and the *lidi* sandbanks offering protection from the Adriatic Sea. At the time, the archipelago, about two and a half miles in length and a mile wide, comprised some 118 islets of various sizes. Some of these islets were elevated above floodwaters and large enough for settlement. Regardless of their size, all were interspersed with mud banks and marshes. Winding through and around the islets were hundreds of natural waterways, some large and some barely rivulets or small streams. Several of the larger channels that were deep enough for boat traffic would become the major canals of the future city of Venice.

The earliest settlements were made on the larger, firmer islands, where a base of clay underlay the mud and reeds on the surface. The inhabitants created further protection from flooding by weaving barriers out of vines and willow branches to keep the water from engulfing the islands. These barriers kept the waves from eroding the islands and could also enclose a marshy area that could then be filled with soil or refuse to create more land.

This lagoon outside Venice resembles the marshland and waterways on which the early city was built.

Many of these settlements were also built on the banks of the larger waterways for ease of transportation and commerce. These original settlements would form the skeleton of the city to come.

EARLY LAGOON SETTLEMENTS

The lagoon islands were populated before the arrival of refugees from the mainland. On the island of Chioggia, the Romans had established a settlement named Clodia, where they produced salt. Salt was an important commodity, used to preserve food and to tan leather. One method of manufacturing salt was by evaporating seawater in the sun in shallow salt pans, which occurred naturally in the southern lagoon near the island. There was also an early Roman settlement on the island of Torcello, where archaeological surveys of the cathedral there have revealed Roman tiles and walkways beneath the present foundations of the church.

There were also a number of fishing villages, with houses built of wattles (rods or stakes interwoven with tree branches or twigs to form walls) and osiers (the tough, flexible branches of willow trees), thatched and mounted on stilts or pilings above the water, each with a front mooring to which the occupants' boat was tied.

The first homes of the refugees would have looked much like this. According to architectural historian Richard Goy: "The earliest houses built in the Venetian lagoon were of timber. They were simple, almost hut-like structures, with timber frames, pitched roofs and a covering of osier thatch from the margins of the lagoon."[4]

THE ISLAND PARISHES

As early settlements grew from isolated clusters of houses to small communities, they were organized into parishes. At the center of each parish was its church, the heart of parish life, which opened onto a village square called a *campo* (field) because such squares were originally large grassy areas much like a village green. In the center of the *campo* was a water well, which was actually a cistern for collecting and storing rainwater for drinking, since the islands had no natural source of freshwater. Most *campos* had direct access to the network of waterways. Next to the parish church was a campanile, or bell tower, whose bells regulated the religious life of the parish by calling members of the community to services or prayers.

Surrounding the *campo* and the church were the homes of the nobility, the richest and most powerful community members, who would become the ruling class of the Venetian Republic. Radiating outward were the homes of the lower classes and their farms and workshops.

The first parish communities were located on the largest and driest islands with access to the largest canal waterways, but as the settlement of the islands increased, parishes grew on the smaller islands and between the older parishes. Later parishes were formed on the periphery of the established areas, until eventually attention turned to developing and consolidating the existing parishes into a greater community.

CREATING CITY STREETS

Venice is one of the few medieval cities that never had a significant Roman settlement on the site first. Most Italian cities were built on the sites of earlier Roman towns, and their streets followed the typical Roman pattern of an organized, regular grid. The streets of Venice, in contrast, were built to connect separate parishes with their maze of tiny, winding paths. As parishes were forced to fit themselves into increasingly limited areas, their boundaries were irregular and their streets did not fit together neatly. Land reclamation, in which wet areas were filled with dirt to create additional land and the adjacent parish islands were suddenly joined, made the map even more haphazard.

Therefore, at parish boundaries, bridges were built across waterways at angles because the streets were out of alignment or the streets themselves led to a dead end at the bank of a waterway. Because Venice had no fast, wheeled traffic, it was not necessary to straighten these streets to accommodate horses or carriages. The streets accommodated only pedestrians since the use of horses was abandoned early in the city's history and the main means of transportation would be the canal system.

BUILDING MATERIALS

As the parishes grew, finding suitable and sufficient building materials meant looking beyond the lagoon. There was very little natural building material available in the marshy flats. Some houses were still being constructed from wood, but overtime inhabitants

EARLY VISITORS TO VENICE

Venice drew visitors even in the very early years of the settlement in the lagoon. One of the earliest was Cassiodorus, who was the prefect, or official, representing King Theodoric the Ostrogoth, who ruled the area at that time. In A.D. 523, after visiting the lagoon, Cassiodorus wrote to the early Venetians from the king's capital at Ravenna. His letter, as quoted in John Julius Norwich's book *A Traveller's Companion to Venice*, provides a clear picture of the lives of these early settlers:

> For you live like sea birds, with your homes dispersed . . . across the surface of the water. The solidity of the earth on which they rest is secured only by osier and wattle [twigs and branches from willow trees]; yet you do not hesitate to oppose so frail a bulwark to the wildness of the sea. Your people have one great wealth—the fish which suffices for them all. All your energies are spent on your salt-fields; in them indeed lies your prosperity, and your power to purchase those things which you have not. Be diligent, therefore, to repair your boats—which, like horses, you keep tied up at the doors of your dwellings.

Just forty-two years later, a military commander of the Roman army also visited the lagoon. The welcome address given by the Venetians, also quoted in Norwich's book, shows that they were already a strong force ready to defend their settlement.

> The Lord, who is our help and protection, has preserved us that we may live in these watery marshes, in our huts of wood and wattle. For this new Venice which we have raised in the lagoons has become a mighty habitation for us, so that we fear no invasion or seizure by any of the Kings or Princes of this world, nor even by the Emperor himself . . . unless they come by sea, and therein lies our strength.

sought to build more permanent dwellings of stone and brick, which had to be transported from the mainland. This was not difficult for the Venetians, who traveled everywhere by water. It was much easier to transport stone to the islands by boat than to carry it in a wagon over potholed, muddy roads.

Venetians enjoyed another advantage in that their buildings did not need defensive features. Since the islands were nearly impossible for potential invaders to approach, there was no need for the city walls, castles, or fortresses found in mainland cities that were always at risk of invasion.

The geology of the lagoon islands, however, required the builders' careful attention to the construction methods used there. The soft, often shifting soil of the islands was unstable. Heavy, inflexible buildings were impossible to build as they would either sink into the soft island structure or crack when the soil shifted.

Under these conditions, brick became the material of choice for Venice's buildings because it is more porous and lighter than stone. During the Roman era there had been a flourishing brick-making industry on the mainland, making use of the excellent clay of the region. The Roman method of brick firing was passed along to the early Venetians, who created the typical dark-red Roman bricks that were flat, tile shaped, and small. Often actual Roman bricks were scavenged from the mainland itself and reused. Layers of the small bricks were adhered with a fairly soft mortar to create walls that could actually withstand structural movement and settling.

Eventually large brick-manufacturing facilities developed in Mestre, located just across the lagoon on the mainland and connected directly to the islands by a waterway. Barges, each typically carrying a load of four thousand to five thousand bricks, were loaded at Mestre's kilns and floated to Venetian building sites. Mestre's brick manufacturers also produced Roman roof tiles from the same clay and the same kilns. Venice thus became an essentially brick-built city.

Bits of Roman stonework, especially decorative fragments and statues, also found their way into Venetian buildings, scavenged from the mainland Roman cities. Often they were brought to the islands by the refugees themselves, who incorporated elements from their mainland homes into their new dwellings. This custom of reusing fragments of older structures

ROMAN BRICKS AND TILE

The Venetians learned their techniques of brick and tile making from the Romans. Bricks were used extensively throughout the Roman world and were of two types: baked and unbaked. Unbaked, sun-dried bricks were common in Rome's eastern provinces and were made from loam or clay that was mixed with straw and chaff and then compacted, usually by treading it with bare feet. This mixture was then molded into bricks that were allowed to dry and harden slowly, sometimes for as long as two years.

Baked bricks were preferred for building large buildings. These bricks were made of clay that was allowed to weather after it was dug from the ground, usually over a winter. Then the clay was treated to remove stones and other impurities, and sand was added to produce the desired color. When the clay was the right consistency, it was patted into wooden molds. These were taken to a drying area to harden before being fired, or baked, in kilns. Roofing tiles were made in the same fashion, except that they were molded into the necessary shapes needed for construction.

Roman bricks and tiles were stamped before firing with the name of the individual or company that made them. Brickyards were often run by the army, by towns, or by private companies. The Venetians would eventually establish their own state brickyards to supply the vast amount of bricks needed to build the city.

The Venetians learned brick making from their Roman neighbors and used baked bricks like these to construct many of Venice's buildings.

Most Venetian buildings are made of brick because it is lighter and more porous than stone.

is known as architectural cannibalism. Many older churches that had been built by earlier inhabitants on other lagoon islands also were stripped by Venetians, who were looking for building materials such as stonework or staircases for their new homes.

As the city grew in importance and wealth, Venetians looked for new sources of stone to create more impressive buildings and monuments. The Istrian peninsula, across the Venetian gulf, had extensive stone quarries located directly on the coast. The stone could easily be transported to Venice in great quantities on barges or in cargo vessels. These quarries were known for a specific type of hard, white limestone often mistaken for marble. It was durable, waterproof, and easy to work with. This stone came to be known as Istrian stone and is found in most of the city's earlier buildings, as it is suited for a large number of uses, such as waterproof foundations, walls, staircases, and decorative stone elements.

Later, marble would also be used, but it had to be imported from the mainland from greater distances and was more expensive. A family could boast of its wealth by using marble on their palace for decorative purposes, and some of Venice's government buildings utilized marble as well, although few buildings would be constructed entirely from it. Sometimes marble was recycled from earlier buildings on other lagoon islands, especially as the Roman cities on the mainland decayed and there was little left to scavenge from them.

Timber remained a basic building material in Venetian foundations, pilings, roof beams, and trusses. The natural pine trees of the Venetian barrier islands were used early in the city's history, but because of the fear that cutting all these trees would lead to the destruction of these protective islands, the remaining trees were carefully conserved. Instead it became necessary to bring in timber from the inland hills of Istria and the northern lands of the Veneto region of the mainland. Great rafts of logs would be floated down the inland rivers, especially the Piave and the Tagliamento, and then to the lagoons and the city. They were then brought ashore at the timber yards of the northern part of the city where they would be sawed into planks and beams.

The final vital ingredient in construction was lime, which, combined with sand and water, made mortar for the bricks and plaster for building interiors. Lime was made by burning limestone in a kiln until it formed quicklime powder. Limestone was found in the hills of the mainland and transported by boat to the city or to the brick-making area of the Mestre, which also had the kilns necessary for making lime. The sand was not taken from the barrier islands as a precaution against erosion. Instead it was produced by dredging the ends of the rivers that fed the lagoon. This not only provided sand but also served to deepen the channels of the rivers and make them more navigable.

SETTLEMENTS BECOME A CITY

Traditional accounts claim that the city of Venice was founded at the stroke of noon on Friday, March 25, A.D. 421, when supposedly three consuls were sent out to the lagoon from the mainland city of Padua to establish a trading post on the Rialto islands. It is

THE LAGOON AS DEFENSE

From the earliest days of settlement, the Venetian lagoon was always the inhabitants' best defense against invaders. After the initial founding of the city by refugees fleeing marauding armies near their mainland homes, the Venetians continued to use the treacherous lagoon waters to their own advantage. They alone knew the safest and deepest channels through the marshes and shallow lagoon waters, and this knowledge was handed down among the inhabitants with the strictest secrecy.

In A.D. 774 the Franks, newly arrived in Italy to drive out the Lombards at the request of the pope, were intent on subduing all of the area, including Venice. Their fleet, led by Pepin, the son of the emperor Charlemagne, sailed into the lagoon from the sea and captured the town of Chioggia and the outer Lido island, from which they would sail to Malamocco, which was the capital of Venice at that time. The Venetians quicky moved the capital to the Rivo Alto islands at the center of the lagoon and then used their knowledge of the lagoon waters to trap the Franks. They lured the Frankish fleet up a narrow channel, which they knew would soon be blocked at one end by the ebbing tide. Then the Venetians drew the Franks out of their boats and onto a low, sandy island where they fought a halfhearted battle until the tide went out, leaving the Frankish boats stranded. More Venetians arrived in special flat-bottomed boats that were perfect for navigating the lagoon waters. They destroyed the Frankish ships, picked up their fellow Venetians, and retreated, leaving the Franks with no way to escape. When the tide came back in, covering the island, most of the Franks drowned.

generally believed, however, that this date is too early for the creation of a permanent city, as many of the inhabitants were still refugees who had not yet made the final move to the lagoon. As time passed, however, the settlement of the islands increased and the parishes multiplied.

By 697, all the settlements of the lagoon were united under an independent military unit ruled by a *dux* (a Roman military chief), or doge, as the position came to be called in the Venetian dialect. Gradually the area of the islands called the Rivo Alto (High Bank), or Rialto, with its direct access to the seaward side of the lagoon, became the center of the emerging republic. The city was called Rivus Altus until around the twelfth century, when it became known as Civitas Venetiarum, and eventually Venetia, the Italian form anglicized as Venice. It became the capital of the lagoon settlements in 810, when the settlements were united against a common enemy, Charlemagne's son Pepin, who attempted unsuccessfully to conquer the city. From then on the parishes expanded and combined into the city-state much as it is today.

Nowhere else is there a city as unchanged from its earliest days as Venice is, mostly due to its isolation from the rest of the world. As the city expanded, this unique location and sense of separation fueled the amazing success of the republic.

THE STRUCTURE
OF VENICE

The tenth century was considered a dark age for all of Europe, when violence and chaos were widespread and there was very little cultural or economic progress. Venice, however, seemed to be immune to these dark times. The city expanded to encompass all of the Rivo Alto islands at the center of the lagoon. As trading increased dramatically, Venice established mainland trading posts, and merchant families began to accumulate large fortunes.

In 997 the doge of Venice, Pietro Orseolo II, attacked a stronghold on the coast of Dalmatia, an area on the eastern edge of the Adriatic in what is now Yugoslavia. A Dalmatian tribe called the Narentines had been raiding the Venetian islands for years, plundering towns and killing people. Once Orseolo captured the strongholds of the Narentines and took control of their territories, much of the Adriatic Sea came under Venetian control. In celebration, the doge sailed his ship near where one of the channels of the lagoon joined the sea. There he poured a glass of wine as a toast to the sea herself in a ceremony that was eventually called the Marriage to the Sea. In this way the Venetians formalized their relationship to the Adriatic, the sea being the source of both wealth and protection. This ceremony is still reenacted in Venice every year.

Three years later, in the year 1000, the Holy Roman Emperor Otto III, the most powerful ruler in Europe, journeyed to Venice to meet with the doge. They established important trading contracts, and Venice gained the prestige and recognition needed to finally establish her as a great European power.

Now a powerful, unified whole, Venice was ready to move from a collection of small parish settlements to a city with its own structure and architecture. As the city grew, it became more and more necessary to develop methods of construction uniquely suited to such a difficult environment.

A LAGOON LEGEND

Of all the stories and legends surrounding the lagoon and its islands, one of the eeriest is the Legend of the Seven Dead Men. In the southwest part of the lagoon is an island called Cason dei Sette Morti, or the House of the Seven Dead Men. The house was an isolated stone building on the island often used by fishermen as a base, as it was often necessary to remain out on the lagoon for several days. They would use the house as a place to eat, sleep, caulk their boats, and mend their nets.

According to the legend, six men and a boy were staying at the house. The men spent the days fishing while the boy remained behind and cooked their meals. One morning the fishermen found the corpse of a man floating in the water, so they hoisted it aboard their boat, planning to take it to the authorities in Venice after breakfast. When the boy saw them approach, he saw the body propped up in the boat and asked them why they did not bring their guest in for breakfast as well.

The other fishermen, coming into the house, decided to play a rather grisly joke on the boy. They told him to go invite the guest himself, cautioning that the man was very deaf and the boy would have to give him a good kick and shout at him to wake him up. Soon the boy returned to the house and began to put breakfast on the table, saying that the guest had awoken and would soon join them. According to Jan Morris in her book *The World of Venice:*

> [The fishermen] stared at each other, say the story-tellers, "pale and aghast"; and presently they heard slow, heavy, squelchy, flabby footsteps on the path outside. The door opened with an eerie creak; the corpse walked in, horribly stiff and bloodless; and by the time he had settled himself ponderously at the table, all those six . . . fishermen had been struck with a lethal chill, and sat before their [food] as dead as mutton. Seven dead men occupied the cason, and only the boy paddled frantically away to tell the tale.

The house is no longer there. Only a pile of brick and stone on an island being consumed by the lagoon are left. But the legend remains.

THE SHAPE OF THE CITY

Other cities in Europe were typically founded as fortified, usually walled, settlements that could be closed off with gates and protected from invasion behind their stone walls. High towers were built for defense and, later, as demonstrations of wealth. When a city's population increased, new walls were built beyond the old ones to accommodate more housing. As these extensive medieval suburbs grew, there was plenty of room for expansion.

Venice, however, developed differently. Fortunately the lagoon and the city's placement on a series of islands meant that defensive walls were not needed. There were fortresses and watchtowers on some of the lagoon islands, and at times there were even chains across some of the waterways that could be used to keep potential invaders out.

More important, Venetians became experts in using limited space in an unusual environment. As Deborah Howard describes in her book *The Architectural History of Venice,*

> Overcrowding was a problem that Venice could do little to remedy, for there was not much scope for expansion on the margins of the city. Whereas in a mainland city such as Florence a series of new walls enclosed progressively larger areas as the city grew, Venice could only grow by the painful process of draining land from the lagoon.[5]

Once the existing islands had been utilized, new land could only be accessed by creating it from the marshes of the lagoon. New ground was made by putting up woven basketwork fences or dikes, high enough to keep the water out as much as possible and then filling behind them with mud dredged from the canals, as well as refuse, gravel from construction sites, street sweepings, and even human waste mixed with sand. Later, dikes would be constructed of green oak pilings and stone. This process was called reclamation, and it was slow and tedious. The resulting land did not have the clay base of the original islands and would never be as stable, but the crowded conditions of the city meant that construction occurred there anyway. Buildings located on these man-made islands were the most likely to crack and lean in time. Venice did have its own suburbs on the Lido islands and eventually on the mainland as well, but space within the city itself was limited and valuable.

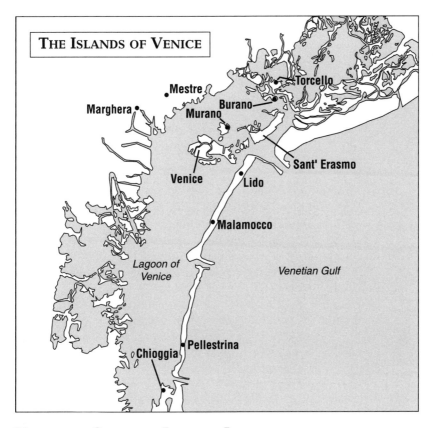

USING THE OUTLYING LAGOON ISLANDS

One of the methods developed for saving space within the city was the use of outlying islands for specific purposes, especially those that would take too much space within the city proper. The island of Murano became the center of the thriving glassmaking industry, largely because of the tremendous risk of fire from the glass-blowing furnaces that could devastate the crowded city of Venice if a fire got out of control there. Burano was a settlement of fishermen and also became a center for lace making. San Michele is still used today as Venice's cemetery island. Other islands were used for leper colonies, to keep the disease away from the city, as well as monasteries, convents, and hostels for the travelers on the Crusades, who often used Venice as their launching point on their way to the Holy Land. Still other islands provided the market gardens that fed the city with fresh vegetables and fruits. Many other industries that first took place in Venice, such as boatyards and timber yards, would eventually find space elsewhere.

WHO IS THE DOGE?

In the year 697, as Venice grew in size and its trading activities became more extensive and profitable, it was decided that a stronger and more efficient government was needed. Representatives of all the communities in the lagoon met in a general council and proclaimed that Venice was a republic. They created a parliament and elected a single head of state, whom they called *dux,* which was the Latin word for "leader." This word was corrupted to *doge* in the Venetian dialect, and to *duke* everywhere else.

Despite the efforts of some political parties to make the position of doge a hereditary office, it continued to be determined by the parliamentary Great Council, a group of fifteen hundred members usually elected from the Venetian aristocracy. The Great Council was the basis for all authority in Venice. In the earliest days of the city, the doge held almost absolute power over the Venetian government. By the fourteenth century, however, a system of checks and balances developed, consisting of the Great Council, a Council of Ten (whose members were elected by the Great Council for six months at a time, and whose three chiefs were confined within the doge's palace during their terms of office), and the doge and his cabinet. This kept the power of the doge in check, making his position that of a figurehead since he could not act without the approval of the other parts of the government.

This left two major centers of Venice, located on opposite sides of the Grand Canal, which snaked its way in a reverse S through the entire city and was its main thoroughfare. The commercial center of Venice was the Rialto, originally named Rivo Alto, and meaning high bank. The Rialto was the marketplace of Europe, where Venetian merchants and bankers built their headquarters. The political center of the city was the Piazza San Marco, or Saint Mark's Plaza. Here the reigning doge lived in his palace, the political life of the city took place, and eventually the prison, mint, and magnificent basilica of Saint Mark would be located.

The remaining city was divided into six districts called *sestieri* (sixths): San Polo, Dorsoduro, and Sante Croce west of the

Grand Canal, and San Marco, Castello, and Canareggio east of the Grand Canal. The houses of the city's ordinary residents, as well as the churches and markets of their parishes and neighborhoods, were located in these districts. As Venice grew, the construction methods in all these districts evolved simultaneously.

BUILDING FOUNDATIONS IN THE LAGOON

Venetians quickly learned that the unique situation of their city on lagoon islands and mudflats would require special construction techniques, which were perfected over the centuries and remained unchanged for much of the city's history. They already had their building materials—brick, mortar, stone, and timber—and the first buildings in the city required little else in the way of special preparations if they were located on firm ground. In these areas, stakes of alder wood approximately forty inches (one meter) long were sunk into the ground. Alder was extremely hard and strong when wet, but it had to remain wet or it would become soft and light. This made it ideal for stakes that would remain in the muddy soil. These stakes supported a horizontal platform called a *zatterone,* or large raft, made of elm and larch woods, which were resistant to repeated cycles of wetting and drying. This platform would support the stone walls of the building's foundation, where brick could not be used because it was not waterproof. As Deborah Howard explains in *The Architectural History of Venice,* "The main principle of Venetian building construction is that the buildings, in effect, were designed to 'float' on the wet sand and mud, in order to resist the constant movement caused by the [ocean's] tides."[6]

As the city spread, however, houses were built in even less ideal conditions. Venice is built on islands created out of sand and silt, and only the firmest islands had a clay layer deep below the soil. For those islands and mudflats without the clay subsoil, the weight of any kind of structure would eventually sink it into this soft ground even if a *zatterone* was used. A more complex solution was found for these buildings. The first step in this process was to construct a cofferdam, a stockade of wooden piles sunk into the soil and lined with wooden planks coated with clay. Excess water would then be siphoned from the area inside the cofferdams, keeping it out of the foundations while construction was taking place. Often a moat was dug around the perimeter of the building site as well, to contain any water that might seep into the foundation area.

To support the stone foundation walls, more piles at least ten feet long and roughly ten inches in diameter were driven into the soil. These pilings were made out of oak, which was extremely hard and tough. To condition them, they were soaked in brackish water before they were used, which kept the wood from splitting as it was being pounded into the soil. The piles were pointed at one end and were pounded into the soft ground by two men using a heavy, two-handled weight or by teams of laborers using heavy hammers. The workers often sang rhythmic beating songs to help them maintain the pounding motion. When longer and longer piles were used in later years, they were driven in by a pile driver, made by hauling a heavy weight up a tall shaft using a system of ropes and pulleys and then letting it drop onto the head of the piling from the top of the shaft. The pilings were sunk in rows or concentric rings beneath the outer walls of what would be the building's foundation, with thinner rows beneath what would be the dividing walls of the interior. The number of pilings used depended on the size and weight of the building being constructed. Underneath older buildings in Venice, the pilings are generally short and widely spaced, but later builders wanted their buildings supported on the hard subsoil of the lagoon islands, and so they used longer pilings closely packed together. These piles remained constantly wet in the soil, which has allowed them to resist decay even into the present time.

Often the central spaces of the foundation would be filled with crushed stone and brick, and then the tops of the pilings were smoothed off about ten feet below the high tide level. They were leveled and packed with special hard clay used only for sealing. This clay was so important that the Venetian government imposed heavy fines on anyone who removed it from the clay pits without a license.

Once the pilings were leveled and sealed, the builders would make a *zatterone* from two layers of larch planks laid at right angles to each other. This would help to distribute the weight of the building across the soft ground. If the load on the *zatterone* was not dispersed evenly, the building would sink or lean.

On top of the *zatterone,* the actual base of the building's walls would be built from white Istrian stone, which could with-

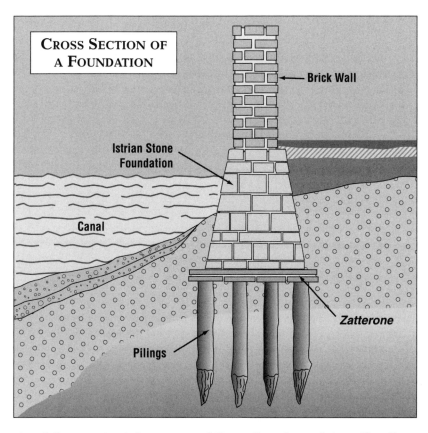

CROSS SECTION OF
A FOUNDATION

Brick Wall

Istrian Stone
Foundation

Canal

Zatterone

Pilings

stand the constant dampness of the soil and any future flooding. If the base layer could not be built entirely from Istrian stone, then it would be faced or coated with a layer of stone and lined inside with clay, also to discourage the dampness of the soil from seeping up into the walls. These first layers of stone were built very thick at the base, to support the weight of the building above, and gradually narrowed as the walls reached the high tide level.

CONSTRUCTION TECHNIQUES FOR VENETIAN BUILDINGS

Once the foundation walls reached ground level, the walls of the actual building were constructed, usually from brick. At first the thin, flat Roman-type bricks were used, or an even thinner brick called a *communella.* By the fifteenth century, Venetian-made bricks were used exclusively, with their distinctive deep-red color and size similar to modern bricks. The walls were made narrower in width as the building's floors rose, from the thickness of three to four bricks at the base to only two bricks at the upper stories, to lessen the weight of the structure.

The roof was usually constructed of terra-cotta roofing tiles, also made in the Roman style. Roman tiles were made in two different shapes: the *tegula,* a flat tile with raised edges, and the *imbrex,* a curved tile that fit over the gaps between the *tegula,* creating a waterproof roof. These tiles were made in the same mainland yards that manufactured the Venetian bricks, and they had the same deep-red color.

Finally, many of the exposed brick walls were coated with a layer of stucco, made of ground terra-cotta tiles mixed with water and slaked lime, which was created from lime partially dissolved with water into a fine powder. A shinier finish could be created by adding granules of Istrian stone to the mixture. Often on more ornate buildings, yet another layer of thin gray plaster was added, and paintings or frescoes were applied to this as decoration. However, in the humid, salty air of Venice, these frescoes did not last very long.

THE POLITICS OF CONSTRUCTION IN VENICE

Just as the buildings of Venice were constructed using specific materials, namely brick, stone, and timber, the actual construction was carried out by specialized groups, or guilds, of workers, who used these materials to build the city. Each guild comprised specialized craftsmen, such as bricklayers, stonecutters, or carpenters. These craftsmen had to serve an apprenticeship of five to seven years in which they learned their craft, usually starting between the ages of twelve and fifteen years old. After their apprenticeship they served as assistants to a guild member for two or three years, until at the end of their training they were tested to prove how well they had learned their craft. Then they were accepted into the guild as full members. Each member maintained his own workshop, where he employed apprentices—his own sons if he had them—and two or three assistants. Any unskilled laborers in the workshop were hired by the day and were not members of the guild.

A Venetian or group of Venetians who wished to erect a building would do their own subcontracting, arranging with various craftsmen to do the work and usually choosing the one who had the lowest estimated price for the job. The builder also had to arrange for the delivery of materials, except in the case of the stonemasons, who supplied their own stone because they best understood what was required for each job. Because the Venetian who wanted to construct the building was responsible for providing materials and managing the project, the individual craftsman needed only to maintain his own workshop and tools

Stonecutters prepare marble for construction. Most Venetian workers specialized in a particular field such as bricklaying, carpentry, or stonecutting.

and did not need a great deal of extra money up front to purchase his own materials or employ other subcontractors.

The guild system helped to ensure that Venice's buildings were constructed with the proven methods that best suited the environment and helped to prevent unsafe conditions from poorly built structures. As Richard Goy notes:

MARCO POLO

One of the most famous Venetians is Marco Polo, adventurer and famous chronicler. He was born in Venice in 1254 to a wealthy family with extensive trading contacts in the East. The Polo family was a good example of the Venetian merchants who were bringing the growing city to greatness. Marco left for the Orient in 1271 with his uncles, crossing regions of the East that would not be seen by Europeans again until the mid–nineteenth century.

Marco liked China and learned the language and customs of the country. He and his uncles held important posts in the Chinese government as well as engaging in trading that made them enormously wealthy.

Eventually the Polos decided to return to their own country. They arrived in Venice in 1295 after an absence totaling twenty-four years. Their relatives did not recognize them right away because they had aged and wore tattered foreign clothing, and they also spoke their native language with great difficulty. However, the men found a way to gain the acknowledgement of their relatives, according to Giovanni Ramusio, as quoted in Fodor's *Exploring Venice:*

> Straightaway they took sharp knives and began to rip up some of the seams and welts [of their clothing], and to take out of them jewels of the greatest value in vast quantities, such as rubies, sapphires, carbuncles, diamonds, and emeralds, which they had stitched up in those dresses in so artful a fashion that nobody could have suspected the fact.

Once the relatives saw these riches, they were happy to claim the Polos as family members.

Although many historic buildings in Venice show considerable evidence of cracking and settlement, this rarely results in serious instability. A number of severe earthquakes over the centuries have resulted in comparatively little damage, certainly far less than would have arisen in a city with more rigid forms of construction. [7]

THE STREETS OF VENICE

As well as requiring special construction techniques best suited to island living, Venice also developed and refined its system of canals, which eventually became the major method of transportation within the city. Jan Morris describes the canals of Venice:

> The central artery of Venice is the Grand Canal, and from that incomparable highway the smaller canals spring like veins, through which the sustenance of the city is pumped daily. . . . There are said to be 177 canals, with a total length of twenty-eight miles. They follow old natural water-courses and meander unpredictably through the city. The Grand Canal is two miles long; it is seventy-six yards wide at its grandest point, and never less than forty. . . . Other Venetian waterways are . . . less imposing—they have an average width of twelve feet, and the average depth of a . . . family bath-tub. One canal goes clean under the church of San Stefano, and you can take a gondola along it if the tide is low; others are so narrow that only the smallest kind of boat can use them. [8]

The canals took over all of the functions that regular streets were used for in other cities, such as transportation and commerce, with boats and barges taking the place of wagons, carriages, and, later, cars and trucks. The canals of Venice rise and fall with the schedule of the tides of the Adriatic Sea, and so also served as the city's sewage and drainage system. Most of the houses in Venice drained their wastewater directly into the canals, where it was flushed away into the lagoon and eventually the sea with every high tide. One fifteenth-century visitor to Venice remarked, "The sea rises and falls there and cleans out the filth from the secret places." [9]

Canals required constant maintenance to keep them from filling in with silt and waste and becoming impassable by boat.

Until the sixteenth century, the lagoon itself was choked with sediment from the several mainland rivers that flowed through it. These rivers were finally diverted to the edges of the lagoon in a massive public works project beginning in 1324 and lasting until 1630. The rivers were diverted into huge canals, which were dug by hand using local workers paid by the Venetians. Digging the canals and removing the soil took nearly 150 years of slow, tedious labor. Later the lagoon was dredged to keep it deep enough for ship traffic.

Canals would be periodically blocked off with small coffer-dams and drained, and the accumulated muck and refuse would be shoveled out and taken by barge to be used in reclaiming new land in the lagoon. Most of the original rivulets of the islands had been built upon so closely that the building foundations formed walls for the canals, and these too would require periodic maintenance. This process would take place every twenty years or so for every canal in a rotation, except for the Grand Canal. It was only dry once in the history of Venice, when a fourteenth-century earthquake swallowed up the waters instantly and left the canal dry for two weeks.

Many of the original canals of Venice have been filled in over the years to create more streets. This was done by blocking off and draining a canal, constructing a wall between it and other waterways, and filling the space with soil and refuse, in the same way that land was reclaimed elsewhere in the lagoon. The area was then paved as a regular street. These streets can be identified by their names: The terms *rio tera* or *piscine* refer to areas that were once canals or small ponds.

A CITY OF BRIDGES

As a city of canals and water, Venice also became a city of bridges in every shape, size, and degree of decoration. At first Venice only had a single bridge across the Grand Canal, located at the Rivo Alto, or Rialto. The original Rialto Bridge was a pontoon bridge that floated on the canal, but at the end of the fourteenth century a permanent wooden bridge was built. In 1450 this bridge came to a dramatic end when it collapsed under the weight of spectators who had gathered there to witness the visit of Emperor Frederick III of Austria. It was rebuilt, again of wood, with a drawbridge at the center and rows of shops on the bridge structure itself. At the end of the sixteenth

The Rialto Bridge spans the Grand Canal. Originally just a pontoon floating on the canal, today's Rialto Bridge is made of stone.

century a contest was conducted among architects to determine a new design, and the Rialto Bridge was replaced with the stone bridge that still stands today.

Other early bridges over the canals of Venice were also made of wood and some exist in the city today, but others were eventually replaced with stone or brick. They usually have a low arch and broad shallow steps. This particular design made possible uses for these bridges that went beyond the simple purpose of crossing water. Deborah Howard describes these early bridges:

> These early stone bridges . . . had no railings at the sides. Until the eighteenth century, rival factions of workers used to have spectacular fistfights on the tops of these

bridges, with many of the less fortunate assailants top-
pling into the water. [10]

The Rialto Bridge remained the only bridge across the Grand
Canal until the 1850s, and residents wishing to cross the canal at
other points would rely on ferries to take them across. It was not
until the occupation of Venice by Napoléon and then the Austrians
that more bridges were added across the Grand Canal.

VENICE AND THE WORLD

The growth of the city on its collection of lagoon islands coincided
with the growth of Venetian shipping and trade. As its stature increased and its influence spread, the city began to enjoy its wealth
and to become more and more concerned with displaying it to the
world. Venice was ready to move beyond the basic structures of
everyday life into the architecture of wealth and power that would
result in some of its most famous buildings.

THE HEART OF
THE CITY

By the year 1000 Venice had established itself as a powerful republic and a leader in world trade and shipping. In 1081 Venice came to the aid of the Byzantine emperor who ruled the vast territories to the east, waging naval battles to keep the Normans from controlling the southern Adriatic and conquering Constantinople. Venice emerged as the victor in these battles and also secured the shipping lanes, making it possible to trade safely with the East. As a reward, the republic also gained trading concessions from the Byzantine emperor, making it exempt from all the taxes and tolls usually imposed in the Byzantine territories. This made it possible for Venetians to combine commerce and industry: They manufactured salt, glass, and wool and sold timber and iron ore from their mainland holdings and then they traded these items with Byzantium and the Orient for luxury items such as spices, olive oil, grain, and wine, which they could not produce for themselves. Because of its geographical location and harbor facilities, Venice became a warehouse for the entire Mediterranean region and was the only place where certain items could be found and goods reordered in large quantities. As a result, Venice enlarged and improved its shipyard, the Arsenale, increasing the rate of construction of ships for its trading fleet and strengthening its naval power. Through these activities, Venetians accumulated vast amounts of wealth and were able to acquire territories beyond their own lagoon.

Another series of events that worked in Venice's favor was the Crusades, in which European Christians waged war on the East in the attempt to regain the Holy Land and the city of Jerusalem from the Muslims who occupied the area. Venice did not join in the battles but instead chose to take advantage of the situation by outfitting the crusaders with ships and supplies and providing staging areas within the city. Venice became the launching spot for the crusaders and made a great deal of money preparing them for their assaults on the Holy Land.

VENICE AND THE CRUSADES

In 1095 the devout Christians of western Europe were out-raged by the Muslim occupation and reported desecration of the Holy Land and the most venerated sites in Jerusalem. They responded to the pope's call to drive the infidels out of the Holy Land and reclaim those sites in the name of Christians, organizing what became known as the First Crusade.

The Venetians did not share this religious fever, but they did resent the piracy and the trade monopolies of the Muslims. They saw the Crusades as a means to let others crush the Muslims and still profit at the same time by leasing Venetian ships, officers, and crews to transport the crusaders to the Holy Land. They charged high rental fees for their navy, established hostels on lagoon islands to house the travelers, and outfitted the crusaders' ships with supplies. The Venetians also benefited by acquiring trading settlements in the East as the crusaders conquered them.

The Fourth Crusade, launched to liberate the Holy Tomb of Christ and which culminated in an attack against Constantinople in 1204, was the most lucrative for the Venetians. The Doge Dandolo, who was ninety-three years old and nearly blind, negotiated the agreement, according to John H. Davis's book *Venice:*

> Venice would furnish transportation for "4,500 horses, 9,000 esquires, 4,500 knights and 20,000 footmen with provisions for nine months." For this the republic was to receive "85,000 silver marks of Cologne," roughly $3,000,000, payable in advance. . . . Of all [related] conquests made on land or sea, "we shall have one half and you the other."

The money was not all paid when the time came for departure, and the Venetians struck a bargain with the crusaders that they could put off payment if they agreed to help the Venetians put down a rebellion in Dalmatia. Once that was accomplished, the Venetian navy and the crusaders decided to attack Constantinople instead of going to the Holy Land. Once the city fell, the crusaders and the Venetians loaded their ships with all the riches they could find and established a new Latin empire there. Many of the treasures looted from Constantinople still adorn Venice today.

As Venice gained influence and importance, the city needed a political and religious centerpiece, a place that would display its growing wealth and prestige and impress foreign visitors. Venetians developed a specific area of their city for this purpose, the Piazza San Marco, *piazza* being the Italian word for an open square or a public place. According to Richard Goy:

> The Piazza San Marco is the heart of Venice, and was for centuries the symbol of the Republic's wealth and stability. Every important event in the [city's] thousand-year history was celebrated (or mourned) here, from ducal coronations to state funerals, from great naval victories to the rituals of the Christian calendar and the festivals of the patron saint. Concentrated at San Marco were the national shrine, the seat of power of the Empire and the official residence of the head of state, the doge. [11]

ESTABLISHING A CITY CENTER

Originally the area now occupied by the piazza was a large and especially firm island, overlooking a deep basin in the lagoon that was a safe anchorage for ships. The first palace of the doge was located here, and historians speculate that it was a small fortified castle with towers and with a small inlet of water on one side that created a sheltered dock for small ships. There was also a small chapel for Venice's original patron saint, Teodoro, or Theodore. A small *campo,* spread out in front of the chapel, with a small canal, the Rio di Batario, on one side. Beyond this was an orchard belonging to a wealthy convent and the ancient church of San Gemignano, which was said to have been established in the sixth century.

Venice, however, was still seeking the respect and recognition of the rest of Europe, and one of the ways Venetians found to gain it was through the acquisition of the body of Saint Mark. Relics were very important to the Christians of that time as a way of gaining prestige, and many churches claimed to have relics of famous saints, such as a finger or an arm bone. Venice took this mania for relics one step further and managed to acquire the entire body of Saint Mark, who was especially important to their city because of the legend that an angel had once visited him as he sailed through the lagoon.

Saint Mark's body was originally housed in an ornate tomb in the city of Alexandria, a seaport in northern Egypt. In the year 828, two Venetian merchants sailed to Alexandria and returned with a body that they claimed belonged to Saint Mark, which they had stolen from his tomb. They smuggled the body out of the city by hiding it in a basket and covering it with pork. Alexandria was a Muslim city and Muslims do not eat pork, so concealing the remains in this way guaranteed that the Muslim customs officials on duty at the port would be disgusted and not look too closely into the basket.

Saint Mark's remains were taken to Venice, and the Venetian rulers decided that a new basilica (church) would be built to house them. They located this new church in the same area as the doge's palace, and Saint Mark displaced Theodore as Venice's patron saint and protector. The construction of the new basilica established the area as Saint Mark's Plaza, the Piazza San Marco.

CONSTRUCTING THE CATHEDRAL OF SAINT MARK

The first basilica that housed the body of Saint Mark was a small chapel and shrine that quickly became a pilgrimage destination for Christians all over Europe who journeyed to Venice to worship at the saint's tomb. This small chapel was built of stone left over from the construction of a nearby abbey as well as some used stone from the island of Torcello and most likely also from Roman ruins on the mainland. The church was shaped like a cross, and where the two sections met, there was a small wooden, domed roof. This chapel was separated from the doge's castle by a narrow canal.

In 976, a fire broke out, destroying several areas of the city and damaging Saint Mark's chapel. Although it was quickly repaired, in 1063 the current doge decided to replace the small chapel with a larger and richer basilica. This rebuilding lasted throughout the reign of three different doges, approximately fifty years. Built mostly from brick, as were most of the buildings in Venice, the new basilica was an enlargement of the old church on the north and south sides. The old chapel of Teodoro (Theodore) was demolished, and a tower that was probably an older corner tower of the doge's palace was incorporated into the rebuilt church. The wooden, domed roof at the center of the cross floor plan was replaced by five great domes with brick vaults.

VENICE AND RELICS

One of the ways in which Venice gained prestige was by collecting religious relics. Nothing gave more legitimacy to a new church than to possess a finger bone or a lock of hair from a saint, and Venice's churches had an amazing number of these relics. The church of San Geremia claimed the body of Saint Lucia, who was martyred in the year 607 and whose body never decomposed. Italy has a long tradition of "incorruptibles," saints and religious people who were believed to be so holy and pure that their bodies did not decay. Scientists suggest this preservation is due to the particular conditions of the crypts beneath the churches and monasteries, whose atmospheric conditions allowed bodies to dry out before decaying.

Venice's most famous relic is the body of Saint Mark himself, smuggled out of Constantinople in a barrel of pork so as to escape the notice of the Muslim officials, who would consider pork to be so offensive that they would not search the barrel. Saint Mark was originally placed in the first of several basilicas built in his honor, which was badly damaged in a fire in 976. A new basilica was built, but when the time came to transfer the saint's body to the new church, the remains could not be found. Some believe the body was consumed in the fire, or that the burial place had been forgotten. In June 1094, however, while the doge and many dignitaries were gathered in the basilica, legend tells that one of Saint Mark's arms suddenly emerged from a pillar on the south side of the church to show that his body rested there. This sacred relic, which scented the air around it with the smell of roses, was moved to the center of the church and placed in a new sarcophagus. Pilgrims came from all over Europe to visit the relic of Saint Mark and show their devotion. The saint's body still rests under the table of the high altar in Saint Mark's Basilica.

Because of construction limitations in Venice, certain types of architectural features were not practical. There were very few domes in the churches and public buildings, for example, because shifting of the soil and the uneven settlement of the ground over time would cause cracking and collapse of any large feature that relies on a rigid structure of walls to support it. Thus domes in Venice had to be small in comparison with those found in other great European churches.

The five brick domes of Saint Mark's Basilica have had structural problems ever since they were built, due to the unstable ground beneath the church. When they were constructed, it was necessary to thicken the walls of the church in order to support their weight, as the domes were created by constructing vaults or arches of brick. Because of their tendency to crack or flatten as the walls of the church shifted, the domes were later repaired by surrounding them with exterior iron rings to help them maintain their shape. These flat domes gave the basilica a Byzantine aspect resembling that of churches in Constantinople and Greece. But in the thirteenth century the exterior of the church was remodeled by adding five taller domes, made of wood and covered with lead, over the older brick domes. These had onion-shaped lanterns on top, and the entire effect was to make the roofline of the church more prominent. At the same time, the relatively plain brick exterior was covered with marble and elaborate ornaments and columns. Ornate mosaics decorated the arches of the porticoes (open colonnades or porches running along the side of the building), including a famous mosaic depicting the arrival of Saint Mark's body in Venice. This is the only original mosaic that still exists on the exterior of the basilica. Patterned marble pavements and floors were also added, replacing the original herringbone-patterned brick floors.

After the Fourth Crusade of 1202–1204, when the Venetians helped to sack the city of Constantinople and carried off many of its treasures, Saint Mark's Basilica was decorated with many architectural elements taken from the East. These items included many multicolored marble columns, placed on the front of the church. Sculptures and fragments of decorative carving taken from Constantinople's buildings were incorporated into the south wall, which was the first facade seen by visitors arriving by sea. Also looted from the East were the famous statues of four gilded bronze horses that are displayed over the entrance to Saint Mark's. The giant statues had been dumped into a corner of the Arsenale (the Venice shipyard) until they were noticed by a nobleman from Florence and placed in their current location. It is unknown whether the horses were Greek or Roman in origin, but it is believed that they were brought to Constantinople by the Romans and for nine hundred years decorated the hippodrome (a large outdoor arena) there. They quickly became a symbol of Venice. In 1379 three Venetian ambassadors went to ask for peace from a Genoese conqueror (who had taken the island of Chioggia), who replied, "Venetians, we shall never make peace with you until we have placed halters on those unbridled horses set on top of the temple of the divine Mark."[12] The horses represented the character of the Venetians themselves, who refused to be subject to anyone else.

By the end of the fifteenth century, the Basilica of Saint Mark had reached its final form, which it still maintains today except for

Over the last one thousand years, Saint Mark's Basilica has evolved from a small chapel into this stone marvel.

the periodic renewal of the faded mosaics. The result is a building with a very un-European feel, a reflection of the influence of Byzantine and Islamic architectural elements that the Venetians brought back with them from their trading relationships in that part of the world.

ENLARGING THE PIAZZA

In 1172 the space surrounding Saint Mark's Basilica and the doge's palace was reorganized to reflect the fact that it was now the hub of a large and thriving city. The Rio di Batario canal was filled in and the orchard beyond it purchased from the convent. The church of

THE PLAGUE

Despite its physical isolation from the rest of the world, Venice twice fell victim to the Black Death, the devastating plague that swept Europe in the 1300s through 1600s and drastically reduced the population. The plague was thought to be spread by infected rats and fleas, so Venice was particularly vulnerable to infection because of its foreign trade. In 1576 the plague struck, emptying the crowds from the Piazza and closing the shops as the population sickened and died. There were so many sick people that the hospital was overflowing and victims were placed on old ships hastily converted to hospitals and towed out into the middle of the lagoon. The population shrank as Venetians either fell sick or fled from the city, and by the time the epidemic was declared over in the summer of 1577, fifty-one thousand Venetians had died, including the famous painter Titian, who was one of the very few victims to receive a formal funeral owing to his status.

In thanks for the city's deliverance from this plague outbreak, the state commissioned a magnificent new church, the Redentore, which is one of five "plague churches" built in Venice as thanks for the city's continued survival.

Another plague swept through the city in 1631, accounting for nearly forty-seven thousand deaths in the city. This time construction was begun on a new church as a prayer for deliverance before the plague epidemic had subsided, resulting in the Santa Maria della Salute, one of Venice's greatest landmarks.

A gondola floats in front of Venice's Palazzo Ducale, the original residence of the doge.

San Gemignano was demolished and rebuilt farther west. This resulted in a huge open square, the Piazza San Marco, approximately six hundred feet in length. A long block of buildings with covered exterior walkways was built on the north side of this square to house the procurators of San Marco, the officials in charge of the saint's shrine in the basilica.

The original residence of the doge, which started as a fortified castle, was transformed into a palace, the Palazzo Ducale. The palazzo now had meeting rooms and ground floor colonnades, with the residence area on the second floor. The Palazzo Ducale was remodeled and decorated in the Byzantine style with a facade of small pieces of pink and white marble and two lower colonnades of Istrian stone. Along the roofline of the palace was a carved and pointed crenellation, which was a decorative stone railing of notched design similar to those found in Muslim mosques in Cairo and Baghdad. Again the Venetians desired to impress visitors to the city who would arrive by sea at the Piazza San Marco.

There were several ornate gateway entrances to the Palazzo Ducale. Two columns located near one entrance to the palace are red in color, and it is said that they were stained crimson by the blood of criminals whose tortured bodies were spread out between them before execution. There are also many statues and pieces of

THE FALL OF THE CAMPANILE

One of the most famous landmarks in Saint Mark's Square, the Campanile, also suffered one of the most spectacular building collapses ever seen in Venice. Supposedly founded in 912, the Campanile served as a bell tower, a lookout over the harbor, and a daytime lighthouse, since its bronze-covered roof was designed to catch and reflect the sun's rays. Like other bell towers in Venice, the 323-foot-high tower was vulnerable to the shifting soil beneath it, despite the legends that the foundations of the tower ran deep beneath the pavement and extended star-shaped in all directions.

In reality, the campanile foundations were gradually weakening. The pilings beneath it were only driven sixty feet deep into the unstable soil, it had been constantly struck by lightning, enlargements and alterations had been made without thought for the tower's stability, and the bricks had been weakened by centuries of weathering. In July 1902, a crack was found in the tower's side. Bands were prevented from playing in the Piazza, and the daily cannon firing that took place in the Piazza was halted for fear that the vibrations it caused would further damage the tower. Unfortunately, these measures did not help, and on July 14, 1902, at 9:52 A.M., the campanile gently collapsed to the ground. A photographer in the square even recorded the event on film.

Amazingly, the nearby Basilica of San Marco was not damaged, and the weather-vane angel that had topped the campanile landed just at the door of the church, which people took as a sign that miraculously the great basilica would not be harmed. All that remained of the campanile was a huge pile of rubble, but the only death was that of a cat that could not be coaxed from the tower.

The remains of the campanile were taken away by barge and dumped into the Adriatic Sea, accompanied by a laurel mourning wreath. Venetians argued about rebuilding the tower, some claiming sculpture of mysterious origin and meaning, also brought back by the Venetians from other countries.

The small inlet of water that once housed small ships was also reclaimed and became the Piazetta, another smaller square at right angles to the larger Piazza. A broad quay, or dock, known as the Molo, was also reclaimed from the lagoon along the front of the Palazzo Ducale to provide a more fitting approach to the square. To add even more prestige to the area, two huge columns of granite were erected as symbolic gateways to the city. Both still stand today, although Venetian legend claims that there was once

that the Piazza looked better without it, but others claimed that the skyline of Venice would never look right again. Finally the decision was made to rebuild the campanile exactly as it had been before and in the same location.

With contributions from all over the world, the campanile was rebuilt, identical to the original but with structural modifications that made it six hundred tons lighter. The foundations were reinforced with one thousand extra pilings, and the tower's bells were recast in a nearby foundry. On April 25, 1912, a thousand years after the founding of the original campanile, the new tower was dedicated and its daily sequence of bell ringing once again measured the hours in the city.

St. Mark's Campanile collapsed in 1902, leaving behind only this pile of rubble.

a third column that fell into the sea and was never recovered. The two columns were topped by statues of Venice's patron saints, the Greek Teodoro and the winged Lion of Saint Mark. Teodoro stands on top of a dragon or crocodile, which he was said to have slain, but the lion statue is actually an ancient Oriental chimera, a mythical fire-breathing creature with the head of a goat, the body of a lion, and the tail of a serpent. The Venetians added wings to this statue to represent the Republic of Saint Mark, but no one knows the origin of the original sculpture.

The Piazza and Piazetta became the center of the city, providing a large space for processionals and state ceremonies, as well as a place to receive foreign visitors, dignitaries, and pilgrims to the shrine of Saint Mark. A large campanile, or bell tower, was erected at the corner of the large and small open spaces. Venetian churches, in light of the instability of the soil, did not have steeples or attached bell towers. Instead, the campaniles were built separately, and over the years, many have started to lean or have actually collapsed due to the shifting ground beneath their foundations.

OTHER BUILDINGS IN THE SQUARE

Venice continued to remodel and rebuild the square over time, mostly to enhance its role as the political and religious center of the city. Where the Merceria, the chief street linking the Piazza San Marco with the Rialto markets, entered the square, a large and ornate clock tower, the Torre dell'Orologio, was built. Its clock face showed the time as well as the signs of the zodiac and the phases of the moon. *"Horas non numero nisi serenus"* claims its legend—"I number only happy hours."[13] Two bronze figures with hammers, known as Moors because their dark color resembles the dark-skinned Eastern people of that name, strike the hours. They were cast in Venice's Arsenale shipyard foundries. The clock mechanism took three years to construct, and the craftsmen responsible for creating it were rewarded with a generous pension. Rival cities spread the rumor that the craftsmen were actually blinded by the Venetians to keep them from constructing a similar work elsewhere. Fynes Moryson, an English traveler to Venice at the end of the sixteenth century, described the clock:

> This tower all covered with marble, beares a remarkeable Clocke, which sheweth the course of the Sunne and the Moone daily . . . and above that the guilded Image of our

The Torre dell'Orologio stands tall in St. Mark's Square. The tower boasts two bronze figures at its top and an ornate clock face.

Lady shineth, placed betweene two doores, out of one of which doores, onely at solemne Feasts, an Angell with a Trumpet, and the three Wise Men of the East following, passé before our Ladies Image, and adore her, and so goe in at the other doore. . . . Upon the very top, two brazen Images, called the Mores, which by turnes striking with a hammer upon a great bell, sound the hours.[14]

The clock tower served as a formal gateway from the marketplace to the Piazza area and accentuated the importance of the church and government buildings found there. The Venetian state library was constructed in 1537, replacing a slumlike area of market stalls and lodgings for pilgrims that had detracted from the rest of the Piazza. The library was constructed to represent the republic as the home of learning and culture and was intended to be the richest and most ornate building since the times of the Greeks and Romans. Unfortunately its ornate vaulted ceiling crashed to the floor soon after construction, and its architect was jailed and later forced to redesign and rebuild the ceiling vaults at his own expense. In addition, a new state mint, the Zecca, was constructed to mint the vast amounts of gold and silver coins now required by the increasingly wealthy republic. Unlike many Venetian buildings with timber frames behind their stone exteriors, the Zecca was constructed entirely of stone, to minimize the risk of fire.

Now all the institutions of the Venetian Republic were housed in one central area of the city, constructed in an appropriate style

A GREAT ESCAPE

In 1755 Giacoma Casanova, one of Venice's most infamous residents because of his reputation as a lover, was jailed in the Venice prison known as the Leads for the lead that covered its walls and roof. The Leads was part of the complex of government buildings located in the Piazza San Marco. It was connected to the doge's palace by the famous Bridge of Sighs, so named supposedly because convicted criminals would stop there and sigh as they looked out at the lagoon before being imprisoned. Casanova was sentenced to five years for repeatedly committing adultery, but as soon as he was imprisoned he began planning an escape.

Casanova found an iron rod in the yard of the prison and turned it into a digging tool. For months he worked at digging a tunnel that would take him out of his cell, only to be moved to another cell before he could finish. Casanova realized that the guards would be watching him more carefully, and so he gave his iron tool to the prisoner in the next cell, a monk named Babi. Babi agreed to dig a tunnel joining their two cells and another to the outside. When he was finished, both prisoners managed to escape, using the iron tool to open doors and gates until they were out. After they arrived in central Venice, Casanova and Babi split up. The police were not able to track them down.

and all harmonizing to create an imposing demonstration of Venice's importance and power. Very few other European cities had this degree of deliberate urban planning, resulting in a completed, unified whole of beautiful proportions. Napoléon would refer to the Piazza San Marco as "the most beautiful drawing-room in Europe, for which it is only fitting that the heavens should serve as ceiling." [15] However, he also destroyed the city's fourteenth-century granaries, a huge brick building located along the lagoon, because it obstructed his view of the lagoon from the Palazzo Ducale. He replaced them with a public garden. Napoléon also demolished the church of San Gemignano in order to make room for a grand ballroom for imperial receptions.

The English author John Ruskin, who spent many hours describing the architecture of Venice, sums up the still impressive effect of the first view of the Piazza San Marco in the 1850s:

> Between those pillars (at the end of the Piazza) there opens a great light, and, in the midst of it, as we advance slowly, the vast tower of Saint Mark seems to lift itself up visibly forth from the level field of chequered stones; and, on each side, the countless arches prolong themselves into ranged symmetry, as if the rugged and irregular houses that pressed together above the dark alley had been struck back into sudden obedience and lovely order. [16]

VENICE AND TRADE

The completion of the Piazza San Marco demonstrated that Venice had reached her peak as a republic and a formidable trading and shipping power. The Piazza represented the strength of the republic's government and culture, while the Arsenale shipyard would represent its military and mercantile power. Venetian merchant ships traveled down the Adriatic Sea to the coasts of Syria, Egypt, and Barbary, northeast to the Black Sea and the Crimea, and westward to Spain, France, Flanders, and England. Although Venice did manufacture goods such as glass, silks, salt, and chemicals, most of her trade came from carrying goods from one foreign port to another. Venetian ships transported precious metals, silk, wax, honey, oil, wheat, wine, cotton, and sugar. Above all, Venetian merchants grew rich by trading in luxury goods from the Orient, such as silks, spices, and perfumes. They also were known to trade slaves.

To maintain their trade monopolies and defend their territories both within the city of Venice and in her growing territories on the mainland, it was necessary for the republic to maintain a large fleet of both trading and military ships. By the year 1423 the Venetian merchant fleet numbered approximately thirty-three hundred ships. Because of the fleet's vital role in the city's livelihood, it was decided that the state would build an official state-run shipyard rather than relying on the services of private boat-building enterprises in the city, enabling officials to control the design and quality of the ships that made up the merchant fleet. This state shipyard became the Arsenale, from the Arabic word *darsina'a,* or place of industry. The Arsenale became the key to Venice's security in trade and defense and the only place by law where the Venetian galley ships could be constructed, according to strict specifications. It also became the largest industrial complex in Europe during its time.

THE CONSTRUCTION OF THE ARSENALE

As early as the year 1100, Venetians had realized that their ships were too valuable to be moored at scattered docks throughout the city where security might be haphazard. The warships and merchant vessels were brought together in a water basin dredged from a natural pond located between two marshy islands on the eastern edge of the city. This basin was connected to the basin of San Marco by a short channel. At first this early version of the Arsenale occupied only eight acres and merely maintained the ships, rather than constructing them. As the focus shifted to ship construction, two rows of shipbuilding sheds were constructed, facing each other across the channel.

By the year 1298, after a recent war against the Genoese that made the construction of more warships necessary, the state decided to enlarge these boatyards. Their territory was expanded to include sites used for rope making and oar making, and a large natural pond to the east of the original shipyard was enclosed. This great basin became the Arsenale Nuovo. The Arsenale became a self-contained fortress, almost a city in itself, for the protection of the Venetian fleet, with convenient access to the deep-water channel leading to the sea. The entire site was enclosed by a high, windowless wall of pink brick, and the only opening was a canal just large enough to allow passage of a single ship. The Arsenale was capable of building, repairing, and outfitting all the ships of the Venetian state.

The chief buildings of the Arsenale were the rows and rows of covered shipbuilding sheds constructed of brick or stone with wooden roofs. These replaced the old open docks so that ships could be built and repaired in all weather. They were high and long enough to leave plenty of room for the workers, and each shed could hold two galleys. By the year 1480 the Arsenale's facilities were large enough to accommodate the construction of 80 ships at one time, and the number eventually grew to 116.

Historian Richard Goy describes the process used to construct ships in the Arsenale:

> The unique Venetian "production line" process origi-
> nated in [the fourteenth century]. New shipbuilding
> sheds were built around the Arsenale Nuovo, but only the

Ships line the docks of the Arsenale, a walled fortress where Venetian warships could be built, repaired, and stored.

keels and hulls [of ships] were constructed here; the hulls were then launched and floated around to the covered docks for completion. Here they proceeded through all the fitting-out stages and were equipped firstly with masts, then with ropes, sails, oars, and weaponry. To support these processes, to the south of the large new basin a specialized zone was developed exclusively for these fitting-out activities; all the departments had water access to the ships on the northern side, while at the back, along their southern flank, an internal street provided vehicular connections.[17]

Eventually the foundries were moved to the Arsenale from their original location in the city so that weapons and cannons could also be manufactured within the shipyards. The Arsenale also manufactured gunpowder, but after two catastrophic explosions that damaged structures and showered the city with debris, it was decided that the gunpowder would be removed from the Arsenale warehouses and stored on two remote islands in the lagoon.

At its peak the Arsenale employed several thousand trained men. Only the finest raw materials were used, mostly wood imported from the Italian mainland, although the storage system in the Arsenale's woodsheds left something to be desired, according to historian Colin Thubron: "Inexplicably, much of the timber was piled in confusion. Even after a special lumberyard had been constructed, the wood was in such disarray that it reputably cost the Arsenale three times as much to find a log as the log was worth."[18]

At its peak of production the workers in the Arsenale could build twenty galleys in half a year. After the ships were built, they were stored in dry dock until needed. In an emergency situation these ships could be fitted out almost as if they were on a conveyor belt. A Spanish traveler, Pero Tafur, described the assembly of a Venetian ship in 1436:

> Out came a galley hull towed by a boat and from the windows they handed out to them, from one the cordage [rope], from another the bread, from another the arms, and from another the ballistae [a weapon that threw

This painted sign identifies a Venetian shipbuilders' guild, one of many groups of skilled men who labored in the Arsenale.

stones or other projectiles] and mortars, and so from all sides everything that was required. In this manner there came out 10 galleys, fully armed, between the hours of three and nine. [19]

This system was the major strength of Venice both as a war machine defending its territories and as a merchant fleet trading all over the world. The Arsenale remained the center of the Venetian economy until it gradually became cheaper to buy ships built by the Dutch.

After Napoléon's capture of Venice in 1797, the French stripped the Arsenale of its weapons and equipment, although it was subsequently modernized and used as a naval base in later years. Today the vast buildings and docks of the Arsenale are vacant, awaiting restoration and reuse, a symbol of the power of Venice at its peak.

4

Building a Palace
in Venice

As Venice became increasingly successful in commerce, the merchant families of the city gained wealth and prestige and began to build palaces that reflected this prosperity. These palaces are called palazzo (the plural form is palazzi) in the Venetian dialect, although before the nineteenth century they were referred to simply as *casae*, or houses, often shortened to *ca'*. The term *palazzo* was at that time reserved for the Palazzo Ducale, the home of the doge. Palazzi are still one of the most identifiable structures that are uniquely Venetian, and at least 397 of them have been identified as being of enough historical and architectural importance to merit restoration. These buildings are difficult to date historically because most were built with the same characteristics and methods, even over a span of hundreds of years. The palaces of Venice, like its other buildings, evolved in a certain way to suit the peculiar conditions of the city and the purposes these residences served.

The Development of the Palazzo

Venice, unlike many other European cities, did not have a specific section of the city where upper-class residences were found. There were no fashionable neighborhoods, and even a location right on the Grand Canal was not always desirable, as many families chose to build on the smaller, side canals of the city. Rich and poor families lived side by side in their particular parishes in the city.

The palazzo was more than a luxury residence; often it served as a place of business as well, with space for merchant families to warehouse goods or do business on the ground floor. Palazzi always had two entrances, one on the water of the canal, and the other opening into the street. This also helped to serve the social and business aspects of the residence. The water entrance, which was considered the principal entrance to the house, sometimes

THE CA' D'ORO

One of the most famous examples of the Venetian palazzo is the Ca' d'Oro, or House of Gold, which was constructed on the Grand Canal beginning in 1421. It has particular value because extensive written records of the process of its construction, kept by its owner, Marino Contarini, a member of one of the most distinguished families in Venice, have survived.

Contarini, according to the standard Venetian practice of the time, demolished an older palazzo on the site in order to build his new palazzo. He arranged for most of the building contractors himself and kept detailed records of who did what jobs, as well as the costs of labor and materials. He also left a description of the original exterior decoration of the palace, which has long since disappeared. The Ca' d'Oro, besides having a wealth of decorative carved stone details around doors, windows, and along the roofline, was once brightly painted. Much of the decorative stone trim work was once gilded with real gold leaf, which is how the palace got its name, and other parts of the exterior walls were painted with two coats of very expensive ultramarine blue. The use of these extravagant materials in an atmosphere as humid and salty as Venice's was a gesture to show how much wealth the family possessed. Even the white Istrian stone was painted with white lead and oil to give the impression of veined marble, and the red marble used was oiled and varnished to bring out the color.

The Ca' d'Oro suffered from later renovations that removed some of the most beautiful elements of the building, but it was restored in the early twentieth century and is now a museum. It is no longer painted in the same bright colors, but the detailed stone carvings still make it one of the most distinctive palazzi on the Grand Canal.

had a quay (a dock) or steps that led directly down to the canal. This facade of the palazzo was also where the owners would showcase their decorating or collection of stone ornaments that may have come as spoils of war from another country. Each palazzo also had an entrance from the street behind the house. These land entrances were usually gated openings set into the high walls of the courtyard, and many of these land gates were remarkably large and richly decorated. The water entrance, however, was still considered to be the formal entrance to the palace.

Every palazzo, like most buildings in Venice, was constructed using the same methods and usually according to a similar floor plan. If a particular family decided to build a new palace to replace an existing palace, they would utilize the same floor plan as the old residence, both as a money-saving technique and as a way to utilize the existing pilings and stone foundations.

THE CHARACTERISTICS OF THE PALAZZO

The Venetian palazzo differs from palaces built in other Italian cities of the time, but all Venetian palazzi, from the earliest palaces all the way to those palaces that were planned but never built because of the collapse of the Venetian Republic in 1797 are remarkably similar. Their features were dictated by their surroundings. The palazzi were built on plots of restricted size because of the space limitations of Venice's islands and the cost and difficulty of reclaiming land from the lagoon. This meant that construction was directed *up* rather than *out*, and most palazzi were

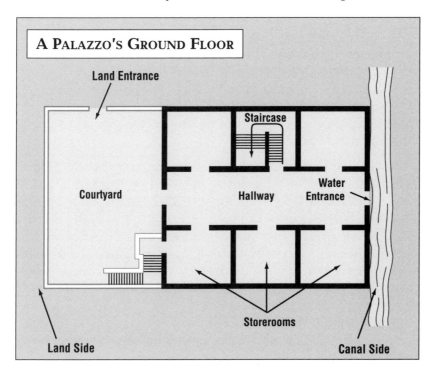

A PALAZZO'S GROUND FLOOR

Land Entrance

Staircase

Courtyard

Hallway

Water Entrance

Storerooms

Land Side

Canal Side

not only built right next to each other but often also shared adjacent side walls. These side walls rarely had windows or decoration.

Space limitations also dictated the shape of the palazzo. Venetian palaces were built in a solid block, without the interior courtyard or patio of palaces in other cities. Any garden area was behind the house and enclosed by a high wall. The water-facing front of the house was the focus, with rows of ornate windows to light the upstairs hallways, balconies (called *pergoli* in Venice), and decorative stonework.

The floor plan of the palazzo was almost always the same as well, no matter who built it or when it was designed. Most of the palaces had a ground floor with a central hallway running down the center from the water entrance gate. Rooms opened off each side of the hallway, usually three on each side. Because many palazzi were owned by merchants who also used them as places of business, these rooms could be used as warehouses and storerooms for merchant goods. Small boats from the fleets of merchant ships would unload their cargoes directly into the main hall of the palazzo's ground floor, where the goods could be easily stored. Peter Lauritzen describes other theories about the use of this ground floor:

> Some misconceptions have grown up around [the ground floor's] use and are frequently repeated. For instance, it is said to have been the space where the gondolas [boats] were stored; but in fact, in the days of the Republic gondolas were always in the water, unless they were being painted or repaired. [20]

Initially all Venetian palazzi had external staircases located in the courtyard at the back of the palace, two flights high with flights at right angles to each other. These staircases were decorated with ornate stonework and carvings. Eventually the palaces came to have inside staircases, but there are still many outside staircases used in Venetian homes. One of the most famous exterior staircases on a Venetian palazzo is the Scala del Bovolo (*bovolo* is the Venetian word for a snail shell), an elaborate spiral staircase with stone ornamentation.

The second floor, or *piano nobile* (grand floor), was the residential area of the house, similar to the first floor because it too had a long central hallway with rooms opening off each side.

The Scala del Bovolo, one of Venice's most famous exterior staircases, is known for its elaborately decorated spiral structure.

Additional floors were built according to how much room the owner needed, with the upper floors less lavishly decorated and usually including an office for the merchant to conduct his business and an attic where servants were housed.

The roof of the palazzo was constructed of wooden timbers covered with Roman roof tiles. And because freshwater was always scarce in the city, the roof was designed to collect rainwater into stone gutters, where it would be channeled down to the cistern or well in the courtyard.

Another unique architectural feature of Venetian palaces was the *altane,* a type of terrace built on the roof. These were especially useful in Venice, with its lack of space for gardens, the poor lighting inside the palace resulting from the lack of windows, and the wonderful views of the city visible from the roofs. The *altane* was a wooden platform supported on brick piers and reached by a rooftop window. It was used for drying laundry, beating carpets, and as a place for Venetian ladies to sit and amuse themselves while they bleached their hair in the sun to make it the fashionable blond color of the time.

The chimneys of Venice, in both the palazzi and the smaller residences, were also unique. Because the risk of fire was so great in a city with a large number of wooden buildings built so closely together, the chimneys were shaped like the smokestacks of train locomotives, opening into a funnel shape. The funnel slowed down the hot air escaping through the chimney, giving the sparks more time to extinguish themselves before they could escape and ignite nearby structures.

A vital characteristic of Venetian palazzi was the location of a well or cistern in the courtyard. Water collection was always a problem for Venice, since the canals carried salt water and were also polluted by the city's sewage. Venice depended on rainwater collected in public wells and cisterns in the city's *campos.* During times of drought, water had to be brought from the mainland in barges. The Venetian palace was no different, as described by Deborah Howard:

> The occupants of private palaces relied on rainwater collected from the rooftop in Istrian-stone gutters, and funneled through glass or terracotta drainpipes within the walls to the well in the courtyard. There it was filtered through sand, and stored in a cistern beneath the courtyard. Cisterns were clay-lined, usually about 3.5 meters [approx-

imately 11.5 feet] deep, and filled with sand for filtration purposes. Water falling onto the paving of the courtyard itself was collected through a series of drains into a small terracotta underground gallery just below the surface, from which it seeped into the cistern below. Empty cisterns could be replenished with fresh water imported by boat.[21]

The wells or cisterns themselves were covered with elaborate wellheads, usually stone columns or elaborate decorative carvings, which were also a distinctively Venetian architectural feature. The city's reliance on these wells for freshwater was so important that there were laws prohibiting beasts, unwashed pots, and unclean hands from touching the water, and deliberately contaminating the water was punishable by death.

To collect fresh drinking water, the Venetians built water wells like this one and covered them with decorated stone columns called wellheads.

LIFE ON A BUILDING SITE

The construction of a palazzo in Venice was a long process that often took many years. In the case of the construction of the Ca' d'Oro, the records kept by the owner have given a fairly accurate picture of what life was like for the workers on the building site.

The amount of work accomplished in a single day was subject to the weather and the amount of daylight available, but generally the workers worked all day with a single break for lunch. Working hours were generally timed by the ringing of one of the huge bells in the campanile of the Piazza San Marco. The workers went home around five o'clock in the winter and seven o'clock in the summer, and although they worked six days a week all year long, there were many festival days and public holidays when they did not have to work.

Rainstorms interrupted bricklaying or plastering and excessively dry weather would cause water shortages that would also make construction difficult. There were also documented incidents of earthquakes that could topple newly built walls, but these were rare.

Disease and illness were some of the greatest hindrances to construction. When the plague appeared, it would often result in the deaths of many workers, but other milder illnesses would mean the loss of a day's pay for the worker and lost productivity for the master builder.

Workers wore a tunic of fairly coarse, long-lasting cloth, with an undershirt during the winter. The tunic was belted and loose fitting, which gave the workers plenty of freedom of movement as they climbed scaffolding and moved around the work site. Most workers wore some kind of hat or cap and hose made of woolen cloth. Shoes were generally soft leather slippers, although leather boots might be worn in bad weather. Most workers also had long, shoulder-length hair and beards.

Fresh water was sometimes in short supply, and the owner of the building being constructed was responsible for providing barrels of wine for the workers, which was usually diluted with water. This was provided for the workers to quench their thirst, not for its alcoholic properties. Building craftsmen were not rich, but most could afford to feed, house, and clothe their families fairly well.

CONSTRUCTING THE PALACE

A merchant who decided to build a new palazzo would first have to locate a site within the city. Often the merchant would purchase an older palazzo and tear it down, reusing the foundations and often the same floor plan in the new structure. Sometimes building materials such as stone or brick would be reused as well. Then the merchant would employ the services of a master builder who established the basic design of the new palace, the arrangements of the structural elements, and how the upper floors would be framed. The palazzo would have the same kind of foundation found in every other building in Venice, with oak pilings sunk into the ground and topped by *zatterone*, but the design of the palace would determine where the pilings would be placed most thickly. It was for this reason that so many merchants reused the foundations of any earlier palace on the site.

The master builder was usually a stonemason. One of his first tasks after designing the blueprint of the palazzo was ordering and arranging the delivery of the necessary stone for construction. Stone was used at the base of the palazzo's walls because of its waterproof properties, with brick taking over on the upper stories because it was lighter and the use of mortar made it more flexible and better able to withstand any movement in the soil beneath the building. Wood was also required for pilings, ceiling timbers, and roof beams, and was also used because it had elastic properties and could shift with changes in the structure. Larch wood was often used for structural elements because it had a larger amount of natural resin and would resist dampness.

The stonemason usually maintained a stonecutting workshop and yard within the city, but most stonework was done on the site of the new palazzo if possible. Sometimes space considerations made this impractical, since there was simply not enough room around the building site to store and cut the stone. The owner of the future palace would usually arrange for the delivery of stone to the site, often by barge from the Istrian coast, although the stonemason would be responsible for picking out the stone best suited for each building application. The owner also had to arrange to provide bricks, sand, lime, and water to the site before any construction could take place. He also would arrange for boatmen to transport heavy cargoes, such as the mud excavated from the canals or the rubble needed to fill the foundation.

If the site did not already have a water cistern from a previous building, this apparatus would have to be constructed first, since water was essential for making the mortar necessary for brick-laying.

When the stonemason had worked out the details of the stone elements of the palazzo, such as the detail around a window, he would create profiles of all the different stone pieces needed for the design, much like puzzle pieces that would fit together to create the whole. The different elements might first be sketched out on parchment, but then they would be taken to the stonemason's workshop and drawn with a stylus onto a bed of damp plaster in a large tray in the center of the workshop. From there, individual sections of the assembly could be made into templates. Templates were patterns that were made out of thin sheets of timber or metals such as zinc, created by a skilled carpenter and then passed to the mason. Templates of stone were carved from the wood or metal models and marked with the name of the stonemason who created them, as well as a code to indicate their placement in the building project. They were usually stored in the stonemason's warehouses after use, in case they were to be reused on another project. Masons had to be highly skilled in both the planning and the actual carving of all the decorative stone elements in a single palazzo.

After the construction of the foundation, the cost of which was often almost a third of the total cost of the house, the bricklayers would begin the actual palace walls, as Goy describes:

> The bricklaying was in fact a simple, straightforward process, involving many large areas of blank wall, with occasional openings for doors and windows, the stonework for which would be inserted later. The total [number of bricks] was perhaps as many as 140,000. Bricks were delivered to the site by the barge-load when required. [22]

On each level, carpenters positioned the wooden beams necessary to support the floors. Floor and ceiling beams were spaced closely together to spread the load more evenly and were nailed to a large horizontal beam set into the inner face of the brick wall. These beams carried much of the weight load of the house and were usually hewn from the trunk of a fully grown larch tree, known for its durability and strength. Sometimes the floor beams

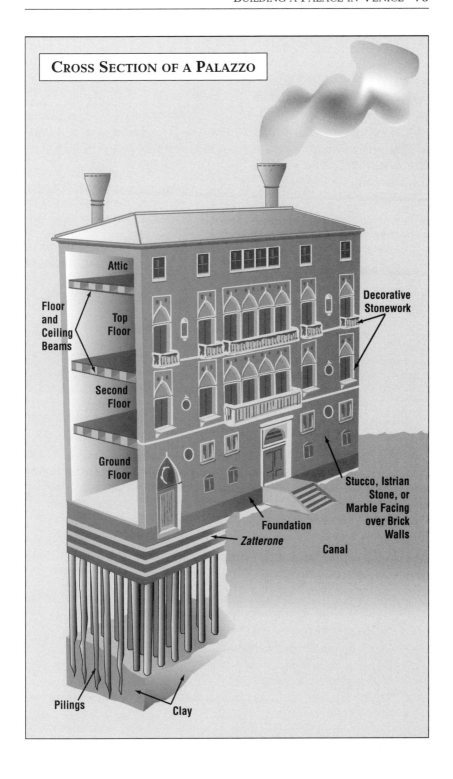

CROSS SECTION OF A PALAZZO

Attic

Floor
and
Ceiling
Beams

Top
Floor

Second
Floor

Ground
Floor

Decorative
Stonework

Stucco, Istrian
Stone, or
Marble Facing
over Brick
Walls

Foundation

Zatterone

Canal

Pilings

Clay

or joists were even attached to blocks of Istrian stone set into the exterior walls of the house and fastened with iron tie-rods. The floor joists were then topped by two layers of wooden planks at right angles to each other.

Wood was also needed for roof construction. The large roof rafters and the smaller cross rafters, called *purlins,* were made from timbers of larch or pine. Roof tiles would be placed on top of this wooden support system.

The final step in palazzo construction was building a dock or quay, if the merchant wanted one. This was done in the same way as a building foundation, where pilings were sunk into the mud, covered with *zatterone* of wood, and then topped with

MAINLAND VILLAS

During the second half of the sixteenth century, the aristocracy of Venice was finally able to spend less time on business pursuits and more time in leisure activities. Many of these wealthy families began to build elaborate villas, or country homes, in the mainland valleys of the Brenta River or in the rolling hills near the Italian Alps. They hired architects such as Andrea Palladio to build some of the most elegant villas in the world, with large formal gardens and manicured lawns, and all the space that they were not able to have surrounding their Venetian palazzi.

Many of these villas were decorated with paintings, frescoes, and sculpture by the most famous artists of the day. These villas were so impressive that wealthy British and American families would imitate them when building their own grand homes, as Thomas Jefferson did when he built Monticello, his Virginia home.

At first these villas were only used during the months of June and July, when the heat of summer would make the lagoon unbearable. By the seventeenth century, however, they were being occupied from April or May through November, and the disciplined businessmen who owned them began to give in to leisurely country living instead of tending to their business affairs in Venice. Some historians believe that this growing inattention to the details of commerce and trade contributed to the downfall of the Venetian Republic.

stone and brickwork to make a pavement at the finished level of the quay.

DECORATING THE PALAZZO

After the basic structure of the palace was completed, the decorative stonework would be applied around windows and doors, in balcony railings, and for other trim work. Many palazzi were very highly decorated, often with a layer of stucco applied over the brickwork and then painted, but these designs did not stand up to the damp climate of Venice, and very few lasted for long. The Ca' d'Oro, a famous Venetian palazzo, was once covered with stucco painted with aquamarine and gold in a show of wealth on the part of its owner. Later palazzi were sometimes encased in a facing of Istrian stone or marble, covering the brickwork completely.

Because of the extensive glassmaking industry in Venice on the island of Murano, many of the palazzi had glass windows, which especially impressed early visitors from other places in Europe where window glass was still rare and oiled canvas or paper were used instead. The glass was usually formed in small circles like the bottoms of glass bottles, held in place within the windows with lead or iron strips and set in wooden window frames.

Once the stone and glasswork were finished, decorative details were applied, especially in interior flooring. In simple homes the floors were made of packed dirt, brick tiles, or wood planks, but fancier flooring was required in the palaces. The first type of flooring was called *pastellon,* ground tiles and brick set into lime mortar and polished to bring out the red color. Often cinnabar, an ore of the metal mercury with a bright red color, was added to the top layer to make the red color even more pronounced. This would be laid on top of the wooden planks of the palazzo's floors. Eventually this was replaced by a more decorative version called terrazzo, a Venetian creation and a very specialized craft, as described by Deborah Howard:

> [Terrazzo] was made up of two layers of crushed brick and stone set in lime mortar, each layer well beaten down with battering rams for several days. Several months had to elapse between the laying of the two layers. The top layer also contained chips of coloured marble, so that when it was smoothed off with mill stones and oiled with

linseed oil the effect was like a random mosaic. As in the case of pastellon, the lime base and tiny stones gave a certain elasticity to the floor surface, so that it could resist minor stresses and strains without cracking. If cracks did appear, it was a fairly simple matter to lay another thin layer of terrazzo on top. Terrazzo floors were so highly polished that one could see one's own reflection in them. [23]

Later terrazzo floors were fashioned with elaborate patterns and borders formed by the mosaic effect of the tiny chips of stone.

PALAZZO STYLES

Although the basic floor plan and characteristics of the palazzo remained the same for most of Venetian history, the exterior decoration and styling did reflect the styles and fashions of particular eras. The earliest palazzi from the twelfth and thirteenth centuries tended to have arched open galleries running the length of the first floor. Gothic palazzi, dating from the thirteenth to fifteenth centuries and the most numerous among all the Venetian palazzi, had elegant arches of Istrian stone and lacelike stone ornamentation. Renaissance palaces from the fifteenth and sixteenth centuries were often built in sandstone instead of brick and incorporated classical elements such as columns of Greek or Roman motifs. Baroque palaces built in the seventeenth century had recessed windows surrounded by rows of columns and ornate carving on every available surface and detail, such as rosettes, garlands, and grotesque, masked faces.

Venetian palazzi are usually remembered not for their designers or builders but by the names of the families that owned and lived in them. It is important to remember that a great number of skilled craftsmen were responsible for the creation of these ornate buildings, which are one of the most memorable features of Venice today. While some of these palazzi have been restored to their original grandeur and often converted to museums, hotels, and offices, still others are in need of structural help to rescue them from collapse.

5

VENICE IN PERIL

As Venice entered the twenty-first century, it had existed on the mudflats and islands of the lagoon for over a thousand years. One of the world's great cities, its fame reflects its unique location, beautiful buildings, and canals. Unfortunately the city is measurably decaying due to several factors, including a rising sea level, the sinking of the city foundations, and the stresses of too many tourists. Even as early as the nineteenth century, the author John Ruskin warned, "The rate at which Venice is going is about that of a lump of sugar in hot tea."[24] This alarming deterioration has led to massive restoration efforts from groups all over the world who desperately want to save Venice.

A LONG, SLOW DECLINE

One of the major contributing factors in the decline of Venice was the fall of the Venetian Republic in 1797. After a thousand years as a republic and a huge trading and military power, Venice's independence came to an end after Napoléon Bonaparte successfully conquered the city.

Napoléon carried out many public works projects in the city, but Venice was subsequently taken over by the Austrians and then eventually became part of the kingdom of Italy in 1866. The changes in government and the resulting lack of regular maintenance in the years following the dissolution of the republic began to take its toll on the city's structures and waterways.

At its peak the government of the Venetian Republic carried out an elaborate system of regular maintenance on the lagoon, the canals, and the buildings of the city. Without human intervention, the lagoon would have long since filled with silt and become just another stretch of the Italian coastline. Instead canals were dug to redirect the rivers of the mainland that previously emptied their loads of silt into the lagoon. In 1534 a massive structure called Saint Mark's Dike was built between the lagoon and the traditional riverbed of the Piave River, to protect the lagoon from the Piave's periodic floods. Finally the Venetians built

Napoléon Bonaparte's army arrives in Venice, precipitating the fall of the Venetian Republic.

huge stone seawalls along the Lido and Pellestrina barrier islands, the long narrow islands that protect the lagoon from the open sea, to keep the fragile islands from being washed away by erosion. These walls would be regularly maintained, but once Venice became part of modern Italy, it is estimated that the Italian government spent the equivalent of only one dollar per yard of seawall per year to maintain all of Venice's sea defenses.

Venice's canals also received regular maintenance during the life of the republic. Canals were periodically drained by the use of small cofferdams, small temporary dams constructed of earth and rocks that blocked the ends of the canal from other canals. Workers would then drain the water from the canal and dredge the accumulated mud, silt, and refuse from the canal bottom. Repairs were made to any walls or foundations revealed during the draining of the canals, and then the cofferdams were removed and the

THE RAILROAD BRIDGE

The railroad causeway bridge, built across the lagoon in 1846, ended Venice's isolation from the rest of the world. Its construction increased the number of tourists to the city by providing them with easier access, causing a boom in the tourist industry and the construction of even more hotels and services.

The idea of a bridge was not a new one. Even during the final days of the Venetian Republic, plans were often drawn up for bridges linking the city to the mainland as a means for increasing trade and limiting the damage done by enemy ship blockades that might prevent access to the Adriatic Sea. Some of these plans called for a causeway with a drawbridge at either end, to maintain some sort of control over access to the city. There were even plans showing a steam train running through the heart of the city to the Santa Marie della Salute, near Saint Mark's Square, which became a classic representation of how industry was threatening Venice.

The railway bridge that was finally built terminates along the Grand Canal, where a church had to be demolished to make room for the train station. It is said that the railroad causeway has chambers to contain explosives if Venice should ever feel threatened and need to sever access from the mainland.

An automobile causeway was added in 1932, but fortunately provisions were never made for accommodating cars in the city itself, and all automobiles must park in multistory parking garages on the outskirts of the city. In the summer the lines of cars stretch back across the causeway, continuing to make automobiles unwelcome in the city on the water.

canal allowed to refill. This maintenance took place constantly in a rotation pattern all over the city, until all the canals had been attended to and the work begun again, a cycle that took about twenty years. Unfortunately this maintenance did not continue in a systematic way after the fall of the republic, and many canals were filled in during the reign of Napoléon and under Austrian control. One of Napoléon's engineers tried to retain the flow of water in some canals by simply roofing them over with arches and building a street above, but in some cases this was unsuccessful due to poor engineering, and there were some dangerous street collapses.

In the twentieth century, however, human manipulation of the lagoon went too far, as described in *The Lagoon of Venice: Environment, Problems, Remedial Measures,* a 1997 scientific conference report:

> During the last century man modified the lagoon system much more intensively: he dug new deep canals for navigation, extended the intertidal flats to provide the necessary areas for a new industrial and urban center, and extended the fish breeding areas, which he protected from the precarious equilibrium of the basin water by dikes. [25]

During a period of thirty years ending in the 1970s, groundwater was being pumped out from deep beneath the city for industrial use. However, the removal of water actually caused the city itself to sink. As Professor Donald R.F. Harleman of the Massachusetts Institute of Technology writes: "Venice is the most sensitive place on earth in terms of the effect of a few centimeters of tidal elevation change. The disastrous decision to pump groundwater from beneath the city, which caused it to sink 11 centimeters, [was] the equivalent of 300 years' worth of natural subsistence. "[26]

The lack of routine maintenance on the structural elements of Venice, combined with the changes made in the interests of shipping and commerce, took its toll on the already fragile city. It was not until a major catastrophe struck the city in 1966 that the Venetians, the Italian government, and the world realized just how precarious Venice's future survival was.

THE FLOOD OF 1966

Venice had long become used to *acqua alta,* or high water, referring to unusually high tides that caused minor flooding in the Pi-

In November 1966, torrential rains flooded Venice's canals, leaving the Palace of the Doges (left) and much of the city underwater.

azza San Marco, the lowest point in the city. Generally Saint Mark's would flood approximately fifty times a year, as compared to seven times a year in 1900 and twenty times a year during the 1950s. But serious flooding was rare in Venice, and it was thought that the old defenses of the seawalls were sufficient against extreme storm tides.

Author Margaret Plant describes the conditions in November 1966 that led to the worst flood Venice has ever known:

> Accounts of the days and nights of 3 and 4 November 1966 tell of the tempest conditions that prevailed through much of Italy, with torrential rain, a sirocco wind [a southeast wind that tends to blow water into the Venetian lagoon] blowing at up to 100 kilometers (approximately 60 miles) an hour and huge seas. Above all, for Venice, the high tide failed to turn at the appointed hour. The sea was driven through the three openings into the lagoon. The island of

VENICE, CALIFORNIA

On July 4, 1905, a man named Abbot Kinney opened a new amusement park and resort on the California coast near Los Angeles. This resort was named Venice, and Kinney carefully planned it to resemble Venice, Italy.

Venice, California, had a network of over two miles of canals dug from the hard, blue clay of the area and lined with concrete. A huge central lagoon at the hub of the canal network served as an outdoor swimming pool eight feet deep at the center. Two thirty-six-inch-diameter pipes connected to the ocean kept the canals and pool supplied with salt water that flowed in and out twice a day with the tides.

All of the buildings in the center of the resort were built in the Venetian Renaissance style of enclosed colonnaded walkways that resembled the buildings in Saint Mark's Square in Italy's Venice. Beautiful new homes lined the canals of the city, which were crossed by picturesque bridges. Public transportation was provided by genuine Italian gondolas on the canals or by a miniature steam railroad. Eventually a huge pier was constructed out into the ocean with an auditorium and café, as well as an amusement park.

During the 1920s, with the rise of the automobile as the preferred form of transportation, the decision was made to fill in most of Venice's canals and the central lagoon in order to create streets. Despite protests by the owners whose homes lined these canals, the canals were filled with dirt in 1929.

Venice is now a part of the city of Los Angeles. The amusement park is gone, but the Venetian-styled downtown buildings still stand as a reminder of what the area was originally intended to imitate.

A boat travels on one of the man-made canals at the Venice amusement park in California.

Sant'Erasmo was submerged to the height of four metres (13 feet); the narrowest point at Pellestrina was deluged as the huge blocks of Istrian stone [the seawall] . . . were dislodged. Locked in the lagoon and driven by an onshore gale, the sea waters flooded the main city to a height of almost two metres and stayed there for twenty consecutive hours. All services were cut; there was total darkness and the real fear . . . that this time the sea would not recede.[27]

All of Venice's electrical and telephone equipment were located roughly two meters (6.5 feet) above the zero water level mark on the tidal gauge at the Basilica de Salute. This gauge was put in place in 1897, at which time the zero mark represented sea level. Sea level is currently nine inches above this zero mark, due to rising sea levels all over the world and the sinking of the city itself. As soon as the 1966 rising tide hit this two-meter level (6.5 feet), the city went black. Fuel tanks holding diesel oil for heating were flooded, turning the water thick, oily, and black. Furniture and household goods from flooded houses floated in the canals, and boats drifted into the narrow streets and were later trapped there when the water receded. Rats climbed the walls of buildings to escape the water, and their carcasses floated in the canals by the thousands. It took a full week to restore power to the city.

There was a worldwide expression of concern following the 1966 flood, as suddenly it was brought to everyone's attention that the treasures of Venice and her buildings were not going to survive much longer unless immediate steps were taken for preservation, restoration, and flood control. It was quickly decided that the flood was not the result of just an unusual set of weather conditions but also because of the measures taken for industry in Marghera: the groundwater pumping that had caused the city to sink, and the new deepened channels in the lagoon for oil tankers. Newspapers all over the world were proclaiming the death of Venice, and international committees were formed to save the city.

THE REASONS FOR VENICE'S HIGH WATER

The increasingly frequent episodes of *acqua alta,* which continue into the present day, cannot be blamed on industry alone. Much of Venice's flooding is due to global warming and its part in increasing the sea level all over the world. Some scientists believe that the earth's temperature has risen by at least 1.1 degrees Fahrenheit over the last one hundred years, although it is not known if this is a normal temperature cycle or due to man-made causes. Because of this rise in temperature, the earth's ice caps have been melting at a higher rate, and sea levels have also risen because of thermal expansion, since water molecules expand when they are heated. This especially impacts those areas like Venice that are very close to the ocean and are vulnerable to any change in water level.

In Venice's case the rising sea levels are coupled with the sinking of the city itself. The pumping of groundwater caused the city to sink drastically, perhaps as much as four inches. As the water beneath the islands was drained, the ground then compacted, similar to a sponge that flattens under pressure when the water is squeezed out. Some of the buildings of Venice that were not built on firm ground have also settled.

The city is believed to be sinking about five inches every century, but this is not a new phenomenon. Archaeologists have found evidence that many of Venice's buildings have had their floors raised many times, and during restoration work in Saint Mark's Piazza, workers discovered five layers of pavement beneath the present layer. The occasional flooding that affects the city is having a drastic impact on the buildings themselves, and this is the biggest concern for preservationists worldwide when they consider the fate of Venice.

THE CRUMBLING BUILDINGS OF VENICE

The original Venetian builders were careful to construct buildings that were suited to the conditions of Venice's unique environment. The lower courses or rows of the foundation walls were made of Istrian stone, which was waterproof and could withstand any rising water from the tides flowing through the ground. Brick was used once the height of the walls was above the water level. This system worked well when there was no motorized boat traffic on the canals. If the sea level rose, the Venetians would adjust the floor levels of their homes accordingly with more layers of stone.

Unfortunately the sea level has been rising, the city has been sinking, and once motorized boats became common on Venice's canals, their wakes, or the waves caused by the boats' motions, have been washing against the foundations of many of the buildings and the side walls of the canals. This washes salt water up to a level above the waterproof stone. The salt water then seeps into the bricks of the walls, which do not have enough time to dry out between high tides and waves. The salt water then dries and the salt crystallizes, breaking apart the structure of the brick itself and causing it to crumble.

At first the deterioration of the brick buildings of Venice was blamed on exotic theories such as the acid from pigeon droppings eating into the brick or even the presence of some sort of

Venice's brick buildings are crumbling, and, in recent decades, wakes from motorized boats have hastened their deterioration.

rock-eating bacteria, but finally it was determined that it was the silent, continual seepage of salt water that was causing the destruction. Green algae was starting to grow on the walls of buildings constantly wetted by the tides, and many residents of Venice moved to the second floors of their homes because the ground floors were damp and moldy from constant flooding. It was time for emergency measures to save the city's buildings, and the flood of 1966 focused international attention on Venice and brought needed assistance.

SAVING VENICE

Some solutions to the erosion of Venice's buildings have been simpler than others. One of the first issues to be tackled was that of motorboats speeding through the canals. Strict fines have been enforced for boats traveling above a posted speed limit, and Venice police use radar-type guns to monitor traffic, especially on the Grand Canal, the busiest waterway in the city. Boat modifications have also been made, according to journalist Catherine Chang:

> The motorboats of Venice create massive waves which erode building foundations and walls. In response, the ACTV (Venice's water transport authority) recently entered into a . . . partnership with a private Venetian company to produce LIUTO's (Low Impact Urban Transport water Omnibus) for its waterbus fleet. Operating since December 1999, LIUTO's minimize the erosive effects of water by generating only low waves. A year later, American entrepreneur Charles Robinson submitted his design for the Mangia Onda (Wave Eater) boat, which not only glides through the water without discernible waves, but also "eats" the waves of other boats. The prototype of the 150-passenger Mangia Onda entered service in November 2000 as an airport shuttle. [28]

Dealing with the problem of boat waves on the canals was only one part of the action needed to save Venice's buildings. The amount of restoration necessary was so great that organizations from different countries began to adopt certain buildings for their own restoration teams. UNESCO, the United Nations Educational, Scientific and Cultural Organization, placed Venice on its list of world heritage sites in need of emergency action. There are now twenty-nine private committees representing nations throughout the world, such as the British organization Venice in Peril and an American group known as Save Venice. Save Venice spent nearly 4 million dollars to restore the fifteenth-century church Santa Maria dei Miracoli, a price much higher than originally estimated because parts of the building would fall apart at the slightest touch, and salt from a canal adjacent to the church had to be removed from the stones.

Individual homes require restoration as well, as described by Lady Frances Clarke, who lives in Venice and whose husband was involved in creating the first British organization dedicated to saving Venice. She found it necessary to repair the crumbling brick walls of her own Venetian home, built alongside a small canal:

> It is very normal to do this system of replacing damp wall through a system called *scuci cuci*, which means to unsew and to sew. You take the old brick out and replace it, section by section, with a special kind of brick made of a special water-resistant consistency. This is the traditional way of doing it. A few feet up, workers place a damp course of impermeable marble that stops saltwater from moving up into the rebuilt wall.[29]

In 1982 Venice formed its own organization dedicated to saving the city, the Consorzio Venezia Nuova, or Consortium for a New Venice, to oversee all activities relating to the lagoon and the edges of the city. The Venetian group Insula is responsible for repairing the city's infrastructure, mostly buildings within the historic center of Venice. Insula workers dredge and repair canals, raise walkways, and lay new utility lines. They rebuild canals by draining them and then replacing broken chunks of the original Istrian stone, which formed the foundations of the buildings built alongside the canals and subsequently became the walls of the canals themselves. They have also rebuilt the steps that lead into the canals and have pumped sealer behind the newly repaired canal walls to keep water from penetrating under the buildings beside the canal. Special cement is used that contains carbon and Kevlar fibers to make it long wearing and temperature resistant. Steel mesh is then laid over the stone wall and coated with a special material that will protect the wall from the wave action of boats in the canal. The president of Insula,

POLLUTION IN THE LAGOON

A significant threat to the canals of Venice is the amount of pollution in the lagoon. The city has always used the natural flushing action of the tides to clean the city's canals of sewage and wastewater, but the lagoon has suffered as a result of pollution from other sources. Agricultural pollution from fertilizer and pesticide runoff enters the lagoon from the mainland rivers. Industrial pollution from Marghera contaminates the lagoon, as well as oil spilled from oil tankers.

The pollution has attacked the animal and plant life of the marshes at the edges of the lagoon that were part of the natural cycles for cleaning the water. During the summer months, algae grows rapidly and then decays in the shallow lagoon waters and in the narrower canals of the city, often resulting in unpleasant gases that can sometimes make inhabitants and tourists sick. Special boats often work in the lagoon, gathering the floating algae on large conveyor belts and disposing of it on lagoon islands.

The environmental organization Greenpeace has been known to give "poison tours" of the lagoon, lasting forty minutes and highlighting sites such as smokestacks and red mold growing on canal banks, which according to Greenpeace can sometimes be a sign of toxic-waste pollution.

A nonprofit organization called the Forum for the Venice Lagoon is working with the University of Minnesota's College of Architecture and Landscape Architecture to try to solve some of the lagoon's pollution problems. Maintaining the ecological balance of the lagoon will be especially vital as the new MOSE flood control project gates are built, affecting the natural flow of the tides in and out of the area.

Building erosion and unhealthy air are just two of the results of rising pollution levels in Venice's canals.

Paolo Gardin, explains: "For thirty years, this city never did anything to maintain the canals. So that is why the work just in the canals will take ten years. After that, there will be regular maintenance— much more regular."[30]

Maintenance and restoration will help remedy many of Venice's structural problems, but the biggest issue still remains: that of the rising sea level and the increasingly frequent flooding that plagues the city. How to best deal with this is one of the most controversial issues in Venice today, and the project under way is one of the most ambitious of any restoration effort.

VENICE AND MOSE

On May 14, 2003, after nearly forty years of debate, the Italian prime minister, Silvio Berlusconi, and the mayor of Venice laid the symbolic cornerstone for a project known as MOSE, named for the biblical figure Moses, who was able to part the seas. "Venice is magnificent, the pride of all Italy," Berlusconi told the media. "Attention to saving this patrimony, this marvel, is at the top of the government's concerns."[31]

MOSE is actually a system of hollow steel gates that can be raised and lowered across the three entrances to the Venetian lagoon, holding back water at times of extremely high tides. When they are not needed, the gates are filled with water and lie flat and invisible against the lagoon floor, allowing normal tides to move in and out of the lagoon. They can be pumped with air and will float into an upright position when needed. There are seventy-eight individual gates in the MOSE system, sixty-five feet wide and up to ninety-two feet high, and they can move independently of each other rather than creating a rigid barrier.

The idea for MOSE came from similar projects built in the Netherlands and on the Thames River in England. Although these gates have been successful, the MOSE project in Venice has raised many controversial questions. Environmentalists are concerned that the gates would have to be used with such frequency that they would disturb the delicate ecological balance in the lagoon, turning it into a stagnant pond. Critics also fear that as sea levels continue to rise, the gates would quickly become useless. Environmentalists advocate raising the levels of the canal walls and quays around the city, as Venetians have done continually over the centuries. But after thirty years of study and ten years of experimentation with scale models of the gates and

THE MOSE FLOODGATES

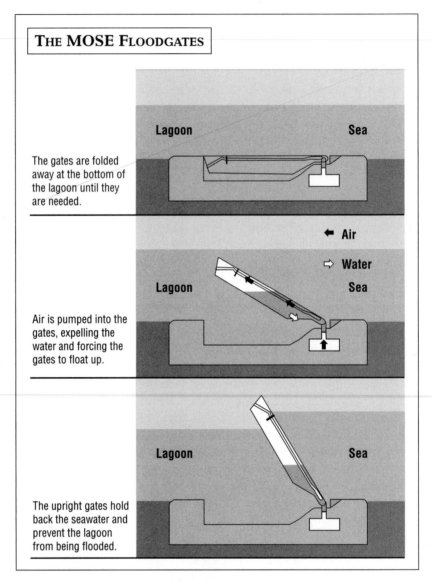

The gates are folded away at the bottom of the lagoon until they are needed.

Air is pumped into the gates, expelling the water and forcing the gates to float up.

The upright gates hold back the seawater and prevent the lagoon from being flooded.

the lagoon, as well as a full-size prototype that was tested in the lagoon itself, the plan has finally been approved by the government and by the Venetian authorities. MOSE will take eight years and over 4 billion dollars to construct. The timing of the project's approval was especially important, since the winter of 2003 set a record for high water levels within the city.

The construction of MOSE will help Venice cope with the continuing problem of high water levels and flooding, but as the city is slowly restored to its former glory, there is one other issue that will determine its fate.

VENICE AND TOURISM

During the rules of Napoléon and the Austrians, Venice had already begun her transformation into a tourist destination, based on elements of her past and her unique history. Bathing establishments and hotels were first built on the Lido islands, named for the *lidi* they border, as ocean bathing became a popular pastime. New hotels and restaurants were constructed in the city as well, and various aristocrats and celebrities began finding their way to the elegant palazzi on the Grand Canal, many of which had fallen into disrepair as their merchant family owners lost

An aerial view of coastal Venice shows the campanile *in Piazza San Marco and the Grand Canal. The city's unique history and beautiful architecture have drawn tourists for centuries.*

their wealth at the fall of the Venetian Republic. Authors came to Venice and wrote about the atmosphere of a city unlike any other in the world, and hordes of travelers found their way based on these writers and the proliferation of guidebooks telling them where to stay and what to see.

Venice is still a popular destination for tourists, but the numbers of people who visit the city daily, especially in the summer, have contributed heavily to the city's problems. Approximately 12 million people a year visit Venice. As the city caters more and more to the needs of tourists, there are fewer of the services needed by regular residents of the city. Prices for everyday goods and housing have risen, and many of Venice's inhabitants have moved to the mainland, where the cost of living is cheaper. In

Tourists crowd Saint Mark's Square. The millions of people who visit Venice each year contribute to the city's pollution and crowding problems.

1938 Venice had a population of 280,000; the city's residents have dropped to just 60,000 today.

"Venice is becoming a beautiful museum and a fine place for the carnival," Professor Gherardo Ortalli of the University of Venice explains. "But it's no longer a real, living city. Try to buy an apple or an orange around St. Mark's—all the shops sell is junk for tourists."[32]

Tourists also produce massive amounts of trash and require increasing numbers of boats for transportation, contributing to the problem of waves from motorboats. Above all, Venetians fear that their city is becoming nothing more than an upscale amusement park, according to Donna Leon, an American novelist living in Venice: "You can't help noticing the change in the quality of life here, the increasing artificiality. The guy who used to sell me bread is gone, and his shop is now a mask store for tourists. Who wants to live in Disneyland? The rate of change is increasing, and I think it's irreversible."[33]

Venice will have to balance tourism with maintaining a real, living city for its inhabitants. As work is done to maintain and restore the city's structures and control flooding, the city will also have to decide how best to deal with the massive numbers of visitors whose presence contributes to the deterioration of Venice. Only a balance between tourism, restoration, and the needs of regular citizens will allow one of the most famous cities on Earth to exist as more than a living museum of its past.

NOTES

Introduction

1. Jan Morris, *The World of Venice*. New York: Harcourt, Brace, 1993, p. 302.

Chapter 1: The Origins of the City

2. John Julius Norwich, ed., *A Traveller's Companion to Venice*, New York: Interlink, 2002, p. 1.

3. Quoted in Arthur Ferrill, "Attila the Hun and the Battle of Chalons," *MHQ: The Quarterly Journal of Military History*, Historical Text Archive. www.historicaltextarchive.com.

4. Richard Goy, *Venice: The City and Its Architecture*. Boston: Phaidon, 1999, p. 46.

Chapter 2: The Structure of Venice

5. Deborah Howard, *The Architectural History of Venice*. Rev. ed. New Haven, CT: Yale University Press, 2002, p. 33.

6. Howard, *The Architectural History of Venice*, p. 56.

7. Goy, *Venice*, p. 49.

8. Morris, *The World of Venice*, p. 117.

9. Quoted in Morris, *The World of Venice*, pp. 119–20.

10. Howard, *The Architectural History of Venice*, p. 45.

Chapter 3: The Heart of the City

11. Goy, *Venice*, p. 60.

12. Quoted in Ettore Vio, ed., *The Basilica of St. Mark in Venice*, New York: Riverside, 1999, p. 74.

13. Tim Jepson, *Fodor's Exploring Venice*. 3rd ed. New York: Fodor's Travel, 2001, p. 131.

14. Quoted in Norwich, ed., *A Traveller's Companion to Venice*, p. 115.

15. Quoted in Jepson, *Fodor's Exploring Venice*, p. 130.

16. Quoted in Goy, *Venice*, p. 60.

17. Goy, *Venice*, p. 77.

18. Colin Thubron, *The Seafarers: The Venetians*. Alexandria, VA: Time-Life, 1980, p. 95.

19. Quoted in Thubron, *The Seafarers*, p. 95.

Chapter 4: Building a Palace in Venice

20. Peter Lauritzen and Alexander Zielcke, *Palaces of Venice*. New York: Dorset, 1978, p. 26.

21. Howard, *The Architectural History of Venice*, p. 67.

22. Richard Goy, *House of Gold: Building a Palace in Medieval Venice.* New York: Cambridge University Press, 1992, pp. 104–105.

23. Howard, *The Architectural History of Venice*, p. 62.

Chapter 5: Venice in Peril

24. Quoted in John Keahey, *Venice Against the Sea: A City Besieged.* New York: St. Martin's, 2002, p. 91.

25. Quoted in Keahey, *Venice Against the Sea*, p. 71.

26. Quoted in Charles Hirshberg, "Venice Sloshes Toward Salvation," *Popular Science*, October 2002, pp. 51–52.

27. Margaret Plant, *Venice: Fragile City 1797–1997.* New Haven, CT: Yale University Press, 2002, p. 355.

28. Catherine Chang, "La Serenissima Is Not Ready to Sleep with the Fishes," April 24, 2001, Harvard Law School, www.law.harvard.edu.

29. Quoted in Keahey, *Venice Against the Sea*, pp. 152–53.

30. Quoted in Keahey, *Venice Against the Sea*, p. 201.

31. Quoted in Associated Press, "Project 'Moses' to Save Venice," May 14, 2003, CNN. www.cnn.com.

32. Quoted in Joseph A. Harriss, "Turning the Tide," *Smithsonian*, September 2002, p. 79.

33. Quoted in Harriss, "Turning the Tide," p. 80.

GLOSSARY

acqua alta: High water or high tides that periodically flood parts of Venice.

altane: A wooden rooftop platform or deck on Venetian buildings.

archipelago: A large group or chain of islands.

Arsenale: The state shipyard of Venice.

basilica: A type of early Christian or medieval church.

Byzantium: The Eastern Roman Empire after A.D. 476, with Constantinople as its capital.

campanile: A freestanding bell tower that accompanies a church.

campo/campi: An open plaza or square, originally a grassy field.

canal: An artificially created waterway for navigation.

cistern: A reservoir or tank for collecting and storing water.

cofferdam: A temporary watertight dam used to keep water out of a construction area.

doge: The head of the Venetian government, from the Latin word *dux,* or leader.

dome: A circular ceiling or roof often used in churches and government buildings.

dredge: To remove sand, mud, or silt from the bottom of a waterway.

estuary: The place where a river's current meets the sea's tide.

facade: The decorative front of a building.

intertidal flats: The mudflats that develop between the high and low tide marks on the lagoon islands.

Istrian stone: A type of white limestone quarried from the Istrian coast on the Adriatic Sea.

lagoon: An area of shallow water separated from the sea by low, sandy islands.

lapis lazuli: A deep blue mineral often used as a pigment for decoration.

lidi: A low, sandy island between a lagoon and the sea.

osier: A tough, flexible twig from a willow tree.

palazzo/palazzi: The Italian word for a palace.

parish: A local church and its surrounding neighborhood.

piazza: A large open square or public space within a city.

piling: A wooden tree trunk pounded into the ground for use as a foundation.

sestieri: The Italian word for "sixths," referring to the six early districts of Venice.

shoal: A sand bank or sand bar in the middle of the lagoon.

terra-cotta: A hard brownish red clay that has been fired in a kiln and is used for building elements.

terrazzo: Mosaic flooring made of bits of stone that are highly polished.

truss: An architectural support such as a beam used to strengthen a structure.

vault: An arched structure that forms the ceiling or roof over a large room or area such as a church.

wattle: Rods or stakes interwoven with tree branches or twigs to make a fence or wall.

FOR FURTHER READING

Books

Mike Corbishley, *The World of Architectural Wonders.* Chicago: NTC/Contemporary, 1996. A look at some of the world's greatest architectural wonders, including Venice.

Cornelia Funke, *The Thief Lord.* New York: Scholastic, 2002. A novel set in Venice with excellent details of the city.

Barrie Kerper, *The Collected Traveler: Venice.* New York: Random House, 2002. A collection of writings about Venice's history and culture.

J.G. Links, *Venice for Pleasure.* 6th ed. London: Pallas Athene, 2000. A classic travel and history guide to Venice.

Lisa St. Aubin de Teran, *Venice: The Four Seasons.* London: Pavilion, 1996. A look at everyday modern life in Venice, with excellent photographs.

Websites

Venezia net s.r.l. (www.doge.it). Provides detailed information on Venice's history, culture, and attractions.

Italian Studies at Emory University (www.emory.edu). Excellent links to Italian and Venetian history.

Venetia (www.venetia.com). The official website of Venice, including history, culture, and travel information.

Europe for Visitors (www.europeforvisitors.com). Provides travel information for Venice, as well as articles relating to the history and current events of the city.

WORKS CONSULTED

Books

Lesley Adkins and Roy A. Adkins, *Handbook to Life in Ancient Rome.* New York: Oxford University Press, 1994. An excellent source of details about life in the ancient Roman world.

Elisabeth Crouzet-Pavan, *Venice Triumphant: The Horizons of a Myth.* Baltimore: Johns Hopkins University Press, 2002. A discussion of the world's images of Venice and the myths surrounding the city.

John H. Davis, *Wonders of Man: Venice.* New York: Newsweek, 1973. A good general overview of Venetian history.

Richard Goy, *House of Gold: Building a Palace in Medieval Venice.* New York: Cambridge University Press, 1992. A detailed study of the construction of the Ca' d'Oro in Venice, based on the original records kept by the builder.

————, *Venice: The City and Its Architecture.* Boston: Phaidon, 1999. An excellent look at the buildings of Venice, their history, and their construction.

Deborah Howard, *The Architectural History of Venice.* Rev. ed. New Haven, CT: Yale University Press, 2002. A comprehensive study of Venice's buildings, with excellent photographs.

Tim Jepson, *Fodor's Exploring Venice.* 3rd ed. New York: Fodor's Travel, 2001. A guidebook to Venice, with history, maps, and photographs.

John Keahey, *Venice Against the Sea: A City Besieged.* New York: St. Martin's, 2002. An overview of Venice's struggles with rising water levels.

Peter Lauritzen and Alexander Zielcke, *Palaces of Venice.* New York: Dorset, 1978. A detailed look at forty-five of Venice's most interesting palaces, their history, and construction techniques.

Jan Morris, *The World of Venice.* New York: Harcourt, Brace, 1993. One of the best travel narratives ever written about Venice.

John Julius Norwich, *A History of Venice.* New York: Random House, 1989. A complete history of the Venetian Republic.

John Julius Norwich, ed., *A Traveller's Companion to Venice.* New York: Interlink, 2002. A collection of writings about Venice from authors throughout history.

Margaret Plant, *Venice: Fragile City 1797–1997.* New Haven, CT: Yale University Press, 2002. A cultural history of Venice in later years, well illustrated.

Colin Thubron, *The Seafarers: The Venetians.* Alexandria, VA: Time-Life, 1980. Covers all the maritime activities of Venice, including shipbuilding, trade, and warfare.

Anthony M. Tung, *Preserving the World's Great Cities.* New York: Random House, 2001. Includes a chapter on the efforts to preserve Venice.

Ettore Vio, ed., *The Basilica of St. Mark in Venice.* New York: Riverside, 1999. A guide to Saint Mark's, including its history and a complete photographic tour.

Alvise Zorzi, *Venice 697–1797: A City, a Republic, an Empire.* Woodstock, NY: Overlook, 1999. A history of Venice with excellent illustrations and details of everyday life.

Periodicals

Albert J. Ammerman, "Probing the Depths of Venice," *Archeology,* July/August 1996.

Joseph A. Harriss, "Turning the Tide," *Smithsonian,* September 2002.

Charles Hirshberg, "Venice Sloshes Toward Salvation," *Popular Science,* October 2002.

Internet Sources

Associated Press, "Project 'Moses' to Save Venice," May 14, 2003, CNN. www.cnn.com.

Catherine Chang, "La Serenissima Is Not Ready to Sleep with the Fishes," April 24, 2001, Harvard Law School. www.law.harvard.edu.

Arthur Ferrill, "Attila the Hun and the Battle of Chalons," *MHQ: The Quarterly Journal of Military History*, Historical Text Archive. www.//historicaltextarchive.com.

Lexi Krock, "Great Escapes: Giacomo Casanova," January 2001, PBS. www.pbs.org.

Elisabetta Povoledo, "Approval of Flood Barriers Won't Settle Controversy," May 22, 2003. Italy Daily. www.italydaily.it.

Jeffrey Stanton, "Venice Construction," 2003, NAID. www.naid. sppsr.ucla.edu.

Video Recordings

The Sinking City of Venice, produced by Marco Visalberghi and Julia Cort. NOVA/WGBH Educational Foundations, 2002.

Venice: The City That Almost Drowned, directed by Rob Swanenburg. Kultur Video, 1999.

INDEX

PICTURE CREDITS

ABOUT THE AUTHOR

Marcia Amidon Lüsted has a degree in English and secondary education, and has worked as a middle school English teacher, a musician, and a bookseller. She lives in Hancock, New Hampshire, with her husband and three sons.